**Subsidizing the Poor:
A Boston Housing Experiment**

Subsidizing the Poor: A Boston Housing Experiment

Joe R. Feagin
Charles Tilly
Constance W. Williams

Lexington Books
D.C. Heath and Company
Lexington, Massachusetts
Toronto   London

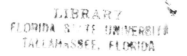
Library of Congress Cataloging in Publication Data

Feagin, Joe R.
  Subsidizing the poor.

  1. Rent subsidies—Boston. I. Tilly, Charles, joint author. II. Williams,
Constance W., joint author. III. Title.
HD7304.B7F4   362.5   72-6712
ISBN 0-669-81844-5

Copyright © 1972 by D.C. Heath and Company.

Published simultaneously in Canada.

Printed in the United States of America.

International Standard Book Number: 0-669-81844-5

Library of Congress Catalog Card Number: 72-6712

Contents

List of Figures

List of Tables

Preface

This book focuses on an experimental rent subsidy program for poor families conducted in Boston during the mid-1960s.[1] The Boston subsidy experiment let a small shaft of light into a very dark corner. From a variety of perspectives—the people, the administrators, and the evaluators—the program actually worked. For the overwhelming majority of the families involved, it provided housing far better than before, housing they liked very much, at a reasonable and competitive cost. In the pages which follow we will present in detail our reasons for drawing these conclusions, the data which lie behind them, our research procedures, and descriptions of the experimental program and its historical and contemporary housing context. In addition, we will examine the broader implications of rent subsidies for the persistent problems of public policy in the area of housing.

A word on terminology is necessary at this point. The terms *rent subsidy* and *rent subsidies* will be used in this book to designate the general type of federal rent support provided for low-income families in the Boston experimental program. The term *rent subsidies* can be viewed as shorthand for the more cumbersome but fully descriptive phrase, "direct rent subsidies paid to landlords in the private housing market to enable low-income families to live in sound housing they could not otherwise afford." *Rent subsidy* here encompasses the type of rent aid for poor families in the experimental Boston program, as well as that in most Rent Supplement and Section 23 Leasing Programs. Technically speaking, the Boston program was termed in the contractual agreements an experimental "rent supplement" program, but we have avoided the use of that term in regard to the Boston program because of its current usage in denoting the more prominent Rent Supplement Program growing out of the 1965 Housing Act. Certainly, we recognize that the term *rent subsidies* can be used in other senses, so that it might cover the federal capital subsidy involved in traditional public housing projects or the subsidies involved in FHA programs for middle-income families. However, in this book we shall generally restrict our usage of the term to those federal rent subsidies paid to private landlords on behalf of *low-income* tenants.

In addition to the authors, several other people took major responsibilities in the research which lies behind this book: Patricia Turner (now Patricia Turner Boyd), who helped plan the inquiry, then organized and directed the earlier phases of the interviewing; James Phillips, who also had a large hand in the interviewing and proved indispensable as a trouble shooter; Sue White, who was a mainstay of our coding and data-processing; Dietrich Garbrecht, who volunteered his services for drafting, mapping, and other crucial tasks; and Karen Ambush, who pitched in on every aspect of the inquiry.

At the Boston Housing Authority, Cornelius J. Connors, Frank Cornell,

Frank Donahue, James Crowley, and Ellis Ash lent us their willing cooperation. At the Boston Redevelopment Authority, we owe our greatest debt to William Richardson. At the Joint Center for Urban Studies, Katherine Bauer, Richard Bolan, Ralph Conant, and Chester Hartman gave us much-needed advice and technical assistance. At the University of Toronto, Ian Lightstone, Muhammad Fiaz, and Abdul Qaiyum Lodhi helped with the preparation of the data, while Jach Wayne and Barry Wellman heckled helpfully. We are also grateful for a number of good ideas which came from Marc Fried and Peter Kranz. Finally, we would like to thank the numerous respondents, black and white, who took time out from their busy lives to help us better understand the housing needs and experiences of Boston's central city residents. We thank them all and hope that the publication of this book will at last compensate them somewhat for their aid.

**Subsidizing the Poor:
A Boston Housing Experiment**

1

The Problem

Introduction

In the preface to the 1968 Housing and Urban Development Act, Congress unequivocally declared its support for the national housing goal of the 1949 Housing Act: "a decent home and a suitable living environment for every American family." Yet the very fact that Congress had to make this reaffirmation nearly two decades after the 1949 Housing Act indicates that the United States still faces a serious housing problem. While the majority of their countrymen prosper in comfortable homes, rats, crowding, and decay continue to surround an incredible number of Americans, particularly nonwhite Americans. During the affluent decades between 1950 and 1970, the general quality of the housing stock was improving rapidly. Even poor people, on the average, saw some improvement in their housing environment. Thus, in the 1950 census over 15 million housing units were counted as seriously substandard, that is, as dilapidated or lacking adequate plumbing facilities. By 1960 the total figure had dropped to 8.5 million housing units, and by 1968 to 4.8 million housing units.

Over these same decades, however, the number of nonwhite families in dwellings which were substandard did not decrease as dramatically as for white families. The total numbers of seriously substandard units for the three points in time were as follows:

Seriously Substandard Housing Units
(in millions)

	White	Nonwhite
1950	12.5	2.8
1960	6.2	2.3
1968	3.2	1.6

In these years whites were escaping in droves from run-down housing. While the number of white households in substandard units dropped 50 percent between 1950 and 1960, the number of nonwhite households in such dwellings declined much more slowly—by only 18 percent. Between 1960 and 1968 the white figure again dropped by nearly half, but the nonwhite figure decreased by only 30 percent. In these decades, a housing market unjust to nonwhite families grew even more unjust. Moreover, if one adds to the nearly 5 million families in seriously substandard housing those families in deteriorating housing, those in

1

overcrowded units, and those paying too much for standard housing, at least as many as 7-8 million families would be part of the American housing problem. This point was underscored by a recent report of the National Commission on Urban Problems:

Visible conditions of building (which the census classifies as *sound, deteriorating,* and *dilapidated*) and plumbing facilities in combination are indeed, as the Census put it, "one measure of housing quality," but only one—and a crude one at that. Quite surely it is on the conservative side—that is, it results in a lower estimate of the volume of substandard housing than most reasonable persons would arrive at on the basis of careful local studies. This seems doubly likely for the housing in older, large, central cities and industrial suburbs of metropolitan areas.[1]

The perilous housing position of many nonwhite families—especially of black Americans and Indians—sums up the effects of both the crucial factors: poverty and color. Poor people of any color face a painful shortage of sound housing within their means; nonwhite poeple of almost any income face discrimination in the housing market.

While the most appalling proportions of inadequate housing appear in depressed rural areas, the central cities of metropolitan areas also have much more than their share. As affluent white America suburbanizes, the central cities move toward a monopoly of old dwellings, racial minorities, and poor people. The men who run the cities and their services therefore find their problems defined increasingly in terms of poverty, segregation, and housing. Naturally, they see that the three are linked: antipoverty drives have implications for segregation and housing, desegregation efforts deal with housing and poverty, housing programs affect segregation and poverty.

If they take housing as their starting point, the designers of public programs face a situation relatively easy to define, rather hard to explain, and exceptionally difficult to change. Substantial minorities in the metropolitan population have no choice but to live in dwellings whose condition menaces their health and welfare. The normal operation of the private market simply does not make available sound housing within their financial means in locations that make sense for their jobs and other daily activities.

Governments have tried a number of ways to supply that sound housing for low-income Americans. Rent controls, antidiscrimination legislation, code enforcement, rehabilitation loans or subsidies, and welfare measures like Aid to Families with Dependent Children all serve as partial correctives within limits set by the existing stock of housing. The guaranteeing of loans for new construction, the writing-down of land seized for urban renewal, and the erection of public housing could add more directly to the stock. Except for low-rent public housing, however, newly-built dwellings supported by the federal government have seldom been within the means of really poor families; planners have therefore had to hope for an efficient trickling down of sound housing to the poor as the well-heeled moved from solid old housing to new dwellings and left vacancies behind them. Even in combination, these diverse measures fall far short of meeting America's housing poverty.

Urban Renewal and the Housing Problem

Urban renewal has put America's housing problem in sharp relief. This federally-sponsored program of urban redevelopment, beginning in earnest in the early 1950s, has not only resulted in a massive domestic program costing billions of tax dollars and touching the lives of millions of Americans but also played a major role in shaping the supply of private and public housing, standard as well as substandard, in urban places.

Ordinarily, city fathers and their planners have concentrated their plans for urban clearance and redevelopment in the city's areas with substantial proportions of rundown housing. Those areas usually contain exceptional numbers of poor people and members of racial minorities. Poor people, particularly the nonwhite poor, literally get pushed around by urban renewal more than the rest of the population. On the whole, they do not obviously gain from the moves they are forced to make. To the extent that seeing one's own physical and social surroundings destroyed and being required to move from one area to another can be reckoned as costs, we might say that the poor and nonwhite families in big cities pay the most for urban renewal, with the least certain return. This sense of the situation, in fact, often shows up in the political controversy over renewal proposals, as homeowners in supposed slums argue that "fair market value" gives them no means of replacing their homes, as owners of neighborhood stores complain they are being driven out of business by relocation, and as civil rights workers point out how regularly urban renewal equals "Negro removal."

Civil rights leaders would have less to complain about if relocation were breaking up involuntary segregation and opening up good housing formerly blocked to black Americans. On the whole, that is not happening. Surprisingly, these sad facts have remained more or less constant for more than thirty years, although in a curious way public attitudes toward them have turned increasingly from approval to disapproval. For example, in 1936 the *Bulletin* of the National Association of Housing Officials published an article headlined "Tenant Relocation in Cleveland."

Another nail has been driven in the coffin of another old anti-housing bugaboo. In light of recent facts, both here and abroad, it has become difficult to convince even the most credulous of certain statements once circulated with great gusto by the opponents of better low-rent housing. No one now believes that coal is stored in bath tubs, nor that most families living in slum or blighted areas won't move into better housing if they have a chance. Very slowly facts are being accumulated that before long will probably dispose of another assertion about slum clearance; that families displaced by such operations are uprooted and scattered throughout the city or metropolitan area, to their own disadvantage and to the detriment of established residential districts.

Some time ago Mr. Howard Whipple Green of Cleveland reported on the relocation of 225 families displaced by the Cedar Central project of PWA. He found that 94% of Negro families and 74% of white families displaced relocated within a mile of their former residences. Last week Mr. Green reported again on the relocation of families moved by the Outwaite housing project, also in Cleveland. The general results are strikingly similar—84% of families relocated within one mile of their former residences. Negro families, who were much more common in the area cleared, moved shorter distances than the white families. 95% of the Negro families relocated within a mile.

These figures, to be sure, indicate some problems and dangers. How long can this process go on without forcing the displaced families into even worse dwellings than those they have lived in? What effect will the coming housing shortage have? Would a similar trend be shown if decent low-rent housing were available elsewhere—possibly in less central and less closely built districts?

The report indicates that the families being displaced by renewal in Cleveland *over three decades ago* were disproportionately black, and intimates that, since the whites moved farther than the blacks, slum clearance either shoved the ghetto into equally rundown adjacent areas or actually consolidated it by removing its few whites. The main change in the message since 1936 is that the tone of self-congratulation has disappeared.

Of course, color and wealth make a big difference in relocation experience as well as in other contacts with the housing market. In his excellent summary of several analyses of relocation, Chester Hartman contrasts the fairly great dispersal of the families relocated from Boston's West End, who were generally whites of low and moderate income, with the frequent en bloc displacement of poor black families from one segregated area to another. He points out that:

Relocation may also have an important effect on the overall residential patterns in the city, particularly since the majority of people displaced by renewal have been Negroes. Depending on the goals of the relocation plan and the nature of relocation services offered to displaced families, the process can be one that fosters dissolution of the racial ghetto or one that perpetuates residential segregation and creates further tensions by rapid population shifts. From the few studies in which these broader questions are discussed, it would appear that relocation efforts have gone no further than dealing with the individual family and its housing problems, with the result that existing patterns of racial segregation have either continued or have become intensified.[2]

Here the question gets complicated. It is clear that relocation offers a strategic moment to strike at involuntary segregation, a moment which has usually been lost. But what about *voluntary* segregation? What about the local attachments which may spring up among people sharing a language or a set of religious beliefs? The aggressive policy of dispersal breaks them up as well as the ghetto. An intelligent relocation policy requires a good deal of knowledge about the nature of local attachments in the metropolis. Work on these questions has already ruled out some bad answers, like the old assumption that slums create and preserve social disorganization, while good housing guarantees satisfactory social life. It has documented the widespread existence of close-knit networks, especially those built around kinship, in urban working-class areas. It has made much clearer what the promising alternative explanations are, and how to test them. But it certainly has not produced solid answers so far.

Relocation is crucial in other ways as well. Forced relocation not only raises questions about minority displacement and resegregation but also about the city housing market and public policy in regard to that market. Relocation has had variable effects—some of them intensely unpleasant—which no one has accounted for, much less predicted, very successfully. One unpleasant effect has been to destroy a significant amount of housing in urban areas. In 1965 Scott Greer commented that "at a cost of more than three billion dollars the urban Renewal Agency (URA) has succeeded in materially reducing the supply of low-cost housing in American cities."[3] Thus the problem of rehousing displaced poor families puts alternative housing policies in sharp relief. Even with the recent drift away from a focus on rehousing the poor toward a greater concern with reviving the central city, general plans for cities often include some housing for low-income families and some ideas on how to make it available to them. When the plan includes clearance or extensive rehabilitation, the renewal authority's responsibility for relocating the displaced poor families even more directly poses a choice among housing policies. Can the private market supply enough sound dwellings at reasonable prices? Will the relocated families have to find places in public housing? Or is there some other viable alternative?

Alternative Housing Policies for Poor Families

Until recently families displaced by urban renewal, highway construction, or other public action have generally faced a choice between unsubsidized housing in the private market and subsidized housing in low-rent public housing (LRPH) projects. Poor relocatees who opted for the private market then either moved into substandard dwellings elsewhere in the city, paid significantly more for their new housing than for the old, or both. This has been about as true of owners as of renters. Those who went to public housing usually have found themselves in large, segregated, institutional developments populated by families who had gone through the same lengthy process of application and screening as they. The experience of the low-income movers in the private market has fed the feeling that urban renewal essentially *displaces* slums instead of eliminating them, and exacts tremendous costs from the helpless on the way. The experience of those who moved to low-rent public housing projects has fostered the accusation that urban renewal segregates the poor and stores them out of sight. While both of these criticisms miss the mark a bit, there is enough truth in them to justify the conclusion that the rehousing of low-income families is the crucial unsolved problem not only of urban renewal but also of public policy in general.

Indeed, until 1959 the federal low-rent public housing (LRPH) program provided the only federally subsidized housing for poor Americans. Still by far the most important low-income housing program, both in terms of dollars spent and persons housed, the LRPH approach began in the mid-1930s under the auspices of New Deal emergency acts and was firmly established by the 1937 Housing Act. The 1949 Housing Act substantially expanded the LRPH program and provided for the construction of 810,000 units in the next six years. These units were never constructed because Congress did not appropriate the funds necessary. Why was this projected amount of low-rent public housing never provided? The reason seems to lie in part in the stigma which came to be attached in the postwar period to federal subsidization of any kind for low-income families—either in the area of welfare or in the area of housing. Moreover, many problems have arisen with public housing, and criticism has been leveled from all sides. One federal commission report on America's housing problem summed it up:

The requirement of local government approval of sites (not to mention problems raised by local referenda and the Workable Program requirement) has restricted the expansion of the program since Public Housing has rarely proved to be a popular neighbor. In addition, housing authorities have been criticized for using authoritarian management policies typified by complex tenant regulations. Surveys indicate that many poor families believe that public housing will not offer them an attractive living environment. Many even prefer to live in unsubsidized, substandard private buildings.[4]

Slowly growing public concern over America's housing problem in the 1960s has stimulated the development of a number of new low- and moderate-income housing programs. In the 1959 and 1961 Housing Acts, Congress adopted two new approaches designed to support construction of housing units by means of federal loans. A Section 202 program provided for low-interest loans to nonprofit developers of rental projects for the disabled and the elderly; and a Section 221 (d) (3) Below-Market-Interest-Rate (BMIR) program allowed the federal lending agency to "purchase mortgage loans made to limited dividend and cooperative, as well as nonprofit, entities at low interest rates based on the average interest paid on outstanding Federal debt."[5]

Subsequently, the important 1965 Housing Act spelled out two additional approaches. One was an expansion of the LRPH program into the area of leased housing, which allowed local housing authorities to lease housing units from private owners and in turn rent them to families who would otherwise qualify for the traditional low-rent public housing. In addition to the Section 23 Leasing Provision, the 1965 Housing Act also established the Rent Supplement Program— the political controversy over which will be discussed in a subsequent chapter. Under this program the rent of individual poor tenants, who were required to pay at least one-quarter of their income for rent, could be directly subsidized in certain types of private housing.

Piling untried new approaches on others just getting underway, the 1968 Housing Act established yet other programs, ostensibly for low- and moderate-income families. The Section 235 Homeownership Program legalized federal support of home purchases by families of moderate income, and the Section 236 Rental Housing Program was designed to replace the earlier 202 and 221 (d) (3) approaches. The subsidization provided was similar; developers of housing projects for moderate-income families could obtain FHA-insured mortgage loans at market interest rates, with the Department of Housing and Urban Development in effect picking up the difference between that interest rate and interest payments at a 1 percent rate. In contrast to the programs in the 1965 Housing Act, these new approaches relied heavily on profit-motivated private developers.[6]

Unfortunately, although the older 221 (d) (3) program and the newer Section 235 and Section 236 programs have sometimes been publicly billed as "low-income" or "lower-income" housing programs, they have in practice served families with incomes significantly above the average incomes of poor families in traditional low-rent public housing. The median income of families in the moderate-income housing programs has in the last few years been approximately $5,000, compared to a median income of less than $3,000 for LRPH families. Consequently, these programs cannot and have not met the needs of most poor families. The Rental Housing and Homeownership Programs are not real alternatives to traditional low-rent public housing, because the limited federal subsidization involved means that housing units generally cannot be rented or sold for sums that families in the LRPH income range could be expected to pay.

Thus the two major federal low-income programs which currently provide workable alternatives to traditional low-rent public housing, and to the substandard private market as well, are the Rent Supplement Program and the Section 23 Leasing Program.

Boston's Experiment with Rent Subsidies

Even before the new Rent Supplement and Section 23 Leasing Programs for low-income families began full-scale operation in the late 1960s, an experimental rent subsidy program in Boston, Massachusetts anticipated many of their most important features and characteristics. In 1964 the Boston Housing Authority (BHA), in conjunction with federal authorities, began to try a housing alternative that many people had discussed, but almost no one had tested: direct rent subsidies for the poor in the private housing market. Up to that point the BHA had put most of its energy into the construction and operation of large public housing developments. As an experiment, its directors decided to provide direct subsidies to forty large low-income families who would otherwise be eligible for the local LRPH program. Financed out of federal funds provided by Congress in the early 1960s for low-income housing experimentation, the Boston program would give preference to families displaced by public action, including urban renewal. Given the fact that most of the Boston Redevelopment Authority's land clearance at that time was going on in the central black ghetto, that meant largely black families. In this particular case, the rent subsidies would permit the families to live in three newly constructed 221 (d) (3) BMIR projects—projects financed by long-term, government-guaranteed, low-interest loans and sponsored by nonprofit organizations with a definite interest in Boston's ghetto housing problems. There they would occupy about one-tenth of the dwellings, while the other tenants in the apartments were to be middle-income families.

The private developers, the landlords, were to receive federally-subsidized monthly checks, handled in this case through the BHA. The tenants were to pay to the private developers the amount they would ordinarily be charged in local low-rent public housing projects, but were to receive new apartments or row houses in one of three newly-constructed developments built primarily for middle-income families. The developers were committed to open occupancy and hoped to have racially integrated populations, despite the fact that two of their apartment developments were in the heart of the ghetto and the third on its edge.

Many people welcomed the novel rent subsidy plan, because the housing of blacks in Boston was a well-known scandal, because the Boston Redevelopment Authority had come under fire for the inadequacy of its relocation efforts, and because the BHA itself had received a good deal of criticism both for the de facto racial segregation of many of its LRPH projects and for its earlier concentration on the construction of large blocks of public housing. Thus, if their costs and social consequences did not work out too badly, direct rent subsidies in the private market promised ways out of these difficulties.

Forty families were not very many compared to the 39,000 dilapidated dwelling units Boston's census-takers counted in 1960, or the 27,000 families reported to have earned less than 3,000 dollars in 1959, or even the 8,000 and more families usually on the waiting list for low-rent public housing. But this small-scale beginning could have large-scale implications. It could begin an entirely new pattern of housing policy. Boosted by the Rent Supplement Provision of the 1965 Housing Act, direct subsidization of the rents of poor families promised to become a major instrument of housing policy even before the returns on the first experiments were in. The forty families therefore deserve attention not only as participants in a crucial experiment, but also as harbingers of future urban housing arrangements and housing policies.

The Evaluation Project

We are here reporting in detail on the Boston housing experiment. Since this experimental rent subsidy program was mainly supported by a demonstration grant from the Housing and Home Finance Agency, the Boston Housing Authority had to arrange for an outside evaluation of its strengths and weaknesses. Ellis Ash, the BHA's director, and his staff felt that the rent subsidy experiment had exceptionally important implications for public policy and provided an unusual opportunity for research. They contacted the M.I.T.-Harvard Joint Center for Urban Studies about conducting the evaluation. As it happened, several people in the Joint Center, and in the departments of M.I.T. and Harvard on which it draws, were working on relevant problems in housing, residential mobility, and social participation. So a research group was formed to undertake the program evaluation, with Charles Tilly taking formal responsibility for its operation.

For several years we watched the program in action, collected information about its background, talked to members of the forty families receiving rent subsidies, and to dozens of other poor families like them but outside the program. Families in several alternative housing groups were carefully interviewed before and after their moves from old housing to new. In following this experiment and these sets of families, we hoped to produce a thorough, detailed evaluation of the promising type of program organized in Boston and some reliable indications of the more general advantages and disadvantages of direct rent subsidies as housing policy. We also hoped to learn something of general value about the housing problems of low-income families, about the impact of relocation on social involvements and everyday life, and about the character of social life in working-class black areas of American cities.

Here are some of the major questions we had in mind as we did our work:

1. What housing alternatives are open to poor black families in Boston, what do they want, what do they get, and how do all of these fit with each other and with the organization of social life in Boston's ghetto?
2. How does the nature of people's local attachments in the city affect how they move, how does it affect their response to moving, and how does relocation—voluntary or involuntary—itself affect local attachments?
3. What happens when low-income and middle-income families move into the same new neighborhoods together?
4. In the experience of the people taking part, how do direct rent subsidies compare with other available ways of acquiring housing?
5. How well did this particular program operate, and how could the use of rent subsidies be improved?
6. What general conclusions, if any, does this experiment suggest for public policy concerning housing, relocation, and the special problems of low-income families? the special problems of black families?

We had no illusion that our study of one experiment would turn up conclusive answers to these large questions. It did not. But it did produce some interesting results which need to be taken into account in answering them.

The chapters that follow present those results. They go from an overview of housing problems in Boston to a summary of the emergence of and controversy over rent subsidization as part of American housing policy; a description of Boston's particular rent subsidy program follows. Then come descriptions of the areas and people most directly involved in the Boston experiment, an analysis of the impact of the program on the people, and systematic comparisons of their experiences with those of families outside the program. The final chapters deal with the organization and administration of the Boston rent subsidy program, implications for public policy, recommendations, and conclusions.

2 The Housing of Boston's Population

Boston and Its Problems

Boston has achieved the reputation of a city that does things about its problems. "Boston Makes a Comeback," announces a national news magazine. "Boston Renewal Stresses Quality and Rehabilitation" is the headline in an engineering publication. And a far-off Canadian newspaper reports "How One City Beat Toronto in Building a New Downtown."[1] "There are still Bostonians rubbed the wrong way by redevelopment . . . ," the newspaper goes on. "These include families and businessmen who have been uprooted, community groups that disagree with specific area plans, simple traditionalists. But the critics appear to be thinning out, as the overwhelming good of the program physically shows itself in the life of the city."

Since our research report deals with some of the "families who have been uprooted," it is worth looking at the urban renewal process shaping their lives. To do so, we must also examine the context—complicated changes in the population, the spatial arrangements, the housing stock, and the public policies prevailing in Boston. All of them help define Boston's housing problems.

In the 1950s the city of Boston had a tired, aged but slowly improving stock of housing, a relatively decrepit downtown, and a tangled transportation system. Its black population was increasing at a moderate pace and concentrating increasingly in a ghetto south of the city's center, while the white population decreased fast enough to produce a decisive net loss of population. From the late 1950s to the middle 1960s the pace of housing change stepped up, through public and private initiative alike. Renewal and highway construction removed many dwellings (standard and substandard) from the supply, many owners improved their small properties, and numerous new apartments shot up. But plenty of rundown buildings remained, and blacks had much more than their share of them. The transportation system saw little improvement, if any. The downtown areas, on the other hand, began a major overhaul; landmarks fell, neighborhoods vanished, skyscrapers rose in their place. Meanwhile, the black population continued to grow, the white population to dwindle, and the total number of people living in Boston, therefore, to decline.

During this time, the segregation of the black population increased. More blacks arrived, whites left predominantly black neighborhoods, few sections of the metropolitan area opened up to black residents, and the displacement of families through urban renewal itself tended to consolidate the ghetto. Although

11

the averages of income, education, housing quality, and other signs of well-being rose for both blacks and whites, the gaps between the two groups remained constant, or even grew. A militant civil-rights movement began to form, the special problems of Boston blacks began to attract attention, and public policy for housing and renewal began to take greater cognizance of those problems. But they did not vanish, by any means. After years of seething without eruption, in June 1967 blacks rioted in Boston. Except that the urban renewal program was better organized and better publicized than elsewhere, the experience of the new Boston had a great deal in common with that of other cities throughout the American Northeast.

The People

Even among the prosperous cities of America's Atlantic coast, metropolitan Boston has a favored population.[2] In 1960, for example, its median reported income of $6,687 and the 53.4 percent of its adult population that had completed high school placed it near the top of the list of American metropolitan areas. Here, however, the distinction between metropolitan Boston and the central city matters. An extraordinarily small proportion—about a quarter—of metropolitan Boston's 2.5 to 3 million people live in the central city. As is true elsewhere, the more privileged tend to live outside, in the metropolitan ring. A simple comparison of the proportion for 1960 of all employed persons in professional and technical occupations makes the contrast clear, and also displays the Boston area's exceptional concentration of these specialized workers:

	Total SMSA	Central Cities	Rings
All SMSA's of the continental United States	12.3%	11.4%	13.3%
All SMSA's from Boston to Washington	12.7	10.7	14.9
New England SMSA's	12.5	10.5	14.2
New York SMSA	12.4	11.1	16.2
Boston SMSA	14.6	11.6	15.8

Although Boston's ring has a substantially higher share of professional and technical workers than the central city, both of them stand high compared with other metropolitan areas. Education gives a similar picture, with the 11.2 percent of metropolitan Boston's adults who were college graduates rising above the metropolitan United States' 8.8 percent, New England's 8.9 percent, and New York's 9.5 percent.

The population stands out in other ways. As American metropolitan areas go,

Boston has a relatively high proportion of people over 65, a low proportion of blacks, many individuals born outside the United States, but a less mobile population than the average.

Yet the population is not immobile. Many of Boston's newcomers, of course, come from elsewhere in Massachusetts and adjoining states. Between 1955 and 1960, the state of New York made by far the largest outside contribution to metropolitan Boston's population. More generally, migration to metropolitan Boston is coming from two sets of states: the coastal band from Maine to Florida and populous, urban states all over the country. Boston, once a great port of entry for overseas migrants of the most diverse origins, now draws mainly on areas with which it has a great deal in common.

The word "migration" often conjures up a picture of poor people arriving in the central city. In fact, migration affects all parts of the metropolis. The people migrating from outside into any particular section of the metropolitan area generally are quite similar to those already there. On the average, the migrants are better educated and more highly skilled than the receiving population. And long-distance migrants actually come to the outlying suburbs more often than to the central city; suburbanites know the site of the cross-country moving van very well. A great deal of the so-called flight to the suburbs is less a movement of families from central Boston to the edge of the metropolitan area than a shuffling of families *among* metropolitan areas.

Yet some flight has occurred within metropolitan Boston; it has left the central sections of the metropolitan area to receive the migrants with the smallest resources and the greatest disadvantages. Most of them, even today, are whites. But the most conspicuous group of migrants to that central area are blacks.

Migration from states to the south is expanding Boston's black population; from 1950 to 1960 the metropolitan area's total went from about 50,000 to about 78,000 blacks. The central city absorbed more than nine-tenths of that increase at the same time it lost some 130,000 whites. At that time, black migrants were coming mainly from the coastal band we have already noticed, especially New York, Virginia, North Carolina, South Carolina, and Georgia. Only their extreme segregation in one part of the central city makes them the most conspicuous minority.

Boston's occupational segregation reinforces its residential segregation. In 1960, nonwhites (a census category which in metropolitan Boston contains very few people who are not blacks) comprised the following percentages of the major male occupational categories:

Professional and technical	1.7%
Managers and proprietors	0.8
Farmers and farm managers	3.0
Sales workers	0.6

Clerical workers	2.3
Craftsmen and foremen	1.8
Operatives	4.4
Private household workers	24.9
Service workers	7.1
Laborers	5.0
Farm labor	2.0

If we use the proportion of all male workers who are blacks—about 3 percent—as a standard of even distribution, then we find both the notorious underrepresentation of blacks in occupations giving higher rewards and some further inconsistencies. Practically no blacks in Boston are sales workers, managers, or proprietors of their own businesses. They are better represented, in fact, among the professions. The largest concentrations of blacks are not among unskilled laborers but among private household workers and other service occupations.[a] The occupational system does not seem to block blacks from jobs where they are in contact with whites, so much as to keep them from positions as equals or bosses of whites. Nor have blacks been able to take the path of small business and private entrepreneurship, by which many European migrants of a half-century ago made their way.

Social Geography

Let us look a little more closely at the geography of the Boston metropolitan population. With over 2,500 persons per square mile, Boston has one of the most densely packed populations of any American metropolitan area. The outsider can sense some of that density by touring the residential sections of Somerville and Cambridge, with their long strings of "three-decker" apartments, or by fighting his way down midtown Washington Street on a shopping day. Yet if he does any more touring, he will also notice enormous variations: 23,000 persons per square mile in Somerville, well over 10,000 in such places as Cambridge, Chelsea, or Malden, around 1,000 in Cohasset or Scituate, closer to 100 in well-heeled suburban areas like Dover or Lincoln.

The high average density does not necessarily mean crowding within dwellings; the metropolitan average of about 0.6 persons per room is rather low. Again we find large variations: from a section of Cambridge where hardly a house has more persons than rooms, to a section of South Boston where a quarter of the dwellings do. And the variations in density or crowding lead us to variations in the social characteristics of the local population.

---

[a]This concentration of blacks in service activities shows up in the classification of the labor force by *industry* as well, in great contrast to the virtual absence of blacks from real estate, finance, insurance, and construction.

Frank Sweetser's handy maps of social characteristics in the Boston area for 1950 and 1960 provide a good starting point for any survey of local variations in population.[3] They show, for example, the larger proportions of young children at the edge of the metropolitan area and the concentrations of older people near the core. They show the rarity of the foreign born at the edge and the concentration of families of Italian stock near the core. They display the particularly high fertility of the western and northwestern suburbs and the large proportions of working women in the city of Boston and its immediate vicinity. And one of the most interesting maps shows the general rise in an index of social rank (combining education and occupation) as one goes out in almost any direction from central Boston, with the greatest mass of high-ranking people due west from the center.

Maps do not do such a good job of showing how groups of characteristics of the population vary together. There are other, less graphic, ways of handling that interesting problem. Sweetser has conducted factor analyses of population and housing characteristics by census tract for the metropolitan area and has come to the conclusion that there are four main dimensions of variation, somewhat independent of each other: socioeconomic status, familism, residential mobility, and ethnicity.[4] Nevertheless, he also concludes that the socioeconomic dimension is by far the most important.

We may take another look at *socioeconomic status* by asking not just which sections of metropolitan Boston have many high-ranking people but which occupational groups tend to live together. Table 2-1 answers this question by presenting rank-order correlation coefficients (statistical measures of association) for each pair of major occupational categories. The occupational categories appear in the table in the order the North-Hatt scheme for assessing occupational prestige assigns to them.

The table expresses a definite rank order. Occupations similar in prestige have high positive correlations; dissimilar occupations, high negative correlations. The private household (that is, domestic) workers, service workers, and the clerical workers keep the order from being neat, surely because the domestic workers often live in, perhaps because many service workers are blacks, and because clerical workers have relatively low incomes. Ability to pay does not account for the general pattern, although it has something to do with it. Metropolitan Boston has sorted out its population into a distinct rank order, in which occupation plays an important part.

We can ask the same kind of question about race and national background. All Bostonians know that the North End has many Italians, Charlestown many Irishmen, Roxbury many blacks. Do we find something like the occupational rank order when we look at the distribution of these groups over the metropolitan area? Do we find an order that corresponds to the sequence in which the largest numbers of these various groups arrived in Boston?[5] Table 2-2 indicates a mixed reply: a rough rank order of education, income, and residential

Table 2-1
Rank-Order Correlation Coefficients (Tau) for Percentages of Employed Males in Major Occupational Categories, over All Census Tracts in the Boston SMSA, 1960

	Professional and Technical Workers	Managers, Proprietors, etc.	Sales Workers	Clerical, etc.	Craftsmen, Foremen, etc.	Operatives, etc.	Service Workers	Nonfarm Laborers
Professional and technical workers	—							
Managers, proprietors, etc.	+.58	—						
Sales workers	+.48	+.59	—					
Clerical, etc.	-.14	-.15	-.09	—				
Craftsmen, foremen, etc.	-.15	-.07	-.03	+.15	—			
Operatives, etc.	-.60	-.50	-.41	+.18	+.18	—		
Service workers	-.30	-.40	-.37	+.22	-.05	+.22	—	
Nonfarm laborers	-.48	-.46	-.43	+.09	+.13	+.48	+.31	—
Private household workers	+.19	+.16	+.11	-.15	-.20	-.20	-.10	-.11
Median income, 1959	6741	7420	5345	4598	5378	4501	3864	3543

Note: SMSA = Standard Metropolitan Statistical Area, a basic census unit.

Table 2-2
Rank-Order Correlation Coefficients (Tau) for Percentages of Total Population in Major Ethnic and Racial Categories, over all Census Tracts in the Boston SMSA, 1960

	Swedish	British	Canadian	Irish	Polish	Italian	Russian	"Other Races"	Black
British	+.37	–							
Canadian	+.25	+.22	–						
Irish	+.02	+.07	+.15	–					
Polish	–.11	–.03	–.08	+.03	–				
Italian	+.01	–.13	+.06	+.05	–.12	–			
Russian	.00	+.11	–.04	–.04	+.37	–.10	–		
"Other Races"	–.07	–.04	–.05	–.05	+.01	–.23	+.12	–	
Black	–.12	–.14	–.08	–.10	+.03	–.16	+.08	+.39	–
Native Stock	+.29	+.27	+.07	–.09	–.12	–.13	–.16	–.18	–.23
Foreign Born	–.24	–.17	–.01	+.15	+.17	+.17	+.19	+.12	+.07
Median Education	+.38	+.36	.00	–.08	–.03	–.20	+.13	–.06	–.17
Median Income	+.35	+.25	+.09	–.04	–.05	+.05	+.01	–.34	–.33

How to Read This Table. Both the headings across the top (the columns) and those down the side (the rows) refer to characteristics of all census tracts in the SMSA: either the percentage of the total population in the category named or, in the last two cases, the median for the tract. To find the relationship of any pair of characteristics, locate the column for one and the row for the other, then look at their junction in the table. The proportions of persons of British and of Swedish stock, for example, show a moderately strong (+.37) tendency to vary together, those of Polish and Swedish stock a slight (–.11) tendency to vary in opposite directions, the proportions of Swedish and Russian stock no relation at all (.00) to each other. The bottom two rows can be read a little differently: persons of Swedish stock are a little more concentrated (+.35) than are persons of British stock (+.25) in tracts with higher levels of income. Or, there is a weak (–.20) tendency for level of education to decline as the proportion of persons of Italian stock rises. The table gives no direct information on the characteristics of the categories of the population themselves.

similarity to the native stock[b] which follows the sequence of migration to some extent, but not nearly the clear internal rank order which appears among the occupational groups. The table takes pairs of the largest categories of race and national background and summarizes their tendency to covary over all tracts of the Boston area. The position of a group in the table follows the closeness of its relationship to the native stock. The correlations average much lower than those for occupation. Swedes and Britons seem to gather to some extent; so do Poles and Russians, blacks and members of other nonwhite races. Otherwise, there are no strong pairs. Nor is the internal ranking consistent.

Such findings could mean that race and national origin do not matter much in the overall sorting of Bostonians into residential areas, or that each racial or ethnic group has its own residential pattern, more or less independent of the others. Which is it?

To get a clearer idea on that question, we must turn to another method. Imagine taking all tracts of the Boston area and ranking them in terms of the share that group X has in their populations. At one end of the rank order for Polish stock, for example, we would find the fourteen tracts where 19 percent of the population is Polish. If group X is spread evenly, not segregated, there will be little progression: few tracts with very low percentages, few tracts with very high percentages. We can draw that pattern as shown in Figure 2-1, Part A.

If group X congregates in some areas, but as a whole mingles freely with the rest of the population, there will still be few tracts with very low percentages of group X, but there will now be some with higher percentages. We can draw that *congregated* pattern as shown in Part B of Figure 2-1.

Finally, if the group is genuinely isolated from the rest of the population, there will be many tracts with tiny proportions of group X, and a few with very high proportions. That *segregated* pattern looks like Part C of Figure 2-1.

Figure 2-2 gives the actual curves for the major ethnic and racial groups of the Boston area in 1960. The reader should note that the logarithmic coordinates in the figures make all the curves less like the segregated pattern than they actually are, in order to make them easier to read. The answer to our earlier question seems to be that ethnicity and race do matter. Some of the categories simply congregate, but some are highly segregated.

The British are at one extreme; their curve looks very much like the ideal "congregation" curve. The Irish, despite local mythology, are not much more concentrated. Blacks, on the other hand, are highly segregated. More than a third of metropolitan Boston's tracts have no blacks at all, four-fifths of the tracts have fewer than two blacks out of every hundred persons, and yet there are six tracts with over 80 percent of their populations black, one of them reaching 95 percent. That is segregation. People of Italian and Russian stock are segregated to quite a degree, but not like blacks. And the numerous Canadians—the area's

---

[b]"Stock" classifies, essentially, the birthplace of the person's grandparents.

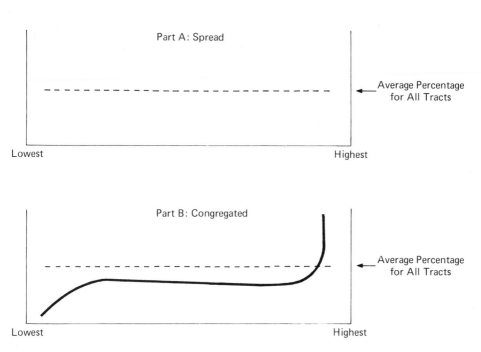

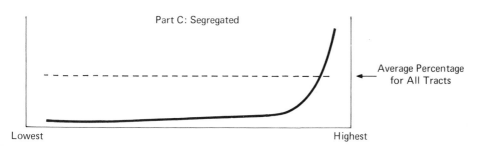

Figure 2-1. Patterns of Racial and Ethnic Distribution.

largest ethnic group—are spread fairly evenly through the metropolitan area, except for a few tracts with Canadian concentrations, almost all of them French Canadian.

Metropolitan Boston's ethnic geography has obviously changed a great deal over the last half-century. The descendents of Irish immigrants have moved out to all sections of the metropolis. Occasional clusters of families of Greek, Lithuanian, or Armenian origin hold only small minorities of the total popula-

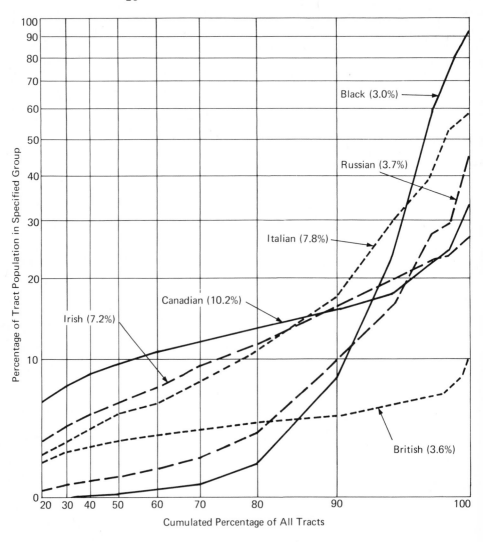

Note: The proportion of any group relative to the entire SMSA is given in the parentheses.

Figure 2-2. Segregation Curves for the Largest Categories of Race and Foreign Stock in the Boston SMSA, 1960.

tions in these categories. Some neighborhoods have changed ethnic character two or three times, and many have lost all ethnic identity. The melting pot has done at least some melting in metropolitan Boston.

Or has it? For the majority who are more than a generation away from other national origins, ethnic ties to a particular neighborhood may not matter so much. The sorting process does bring together neighbors who are similar in occupation, education, and income. Yet ethnic divisions survive. Immigrants and their children still cluster. The segregation curves set off metropolitan Boston's Poles, Italians, and Russians from the rest of the population. For members of these groups, congregation, or even segregation, by national background may be more significant than division by social class.

The graphs for occupational groups strengthen that impression (Figures 2-3 and 2-4). All the occupational curves resemble the "congregation" model more than the "segregation" model. The small category "private household workers"

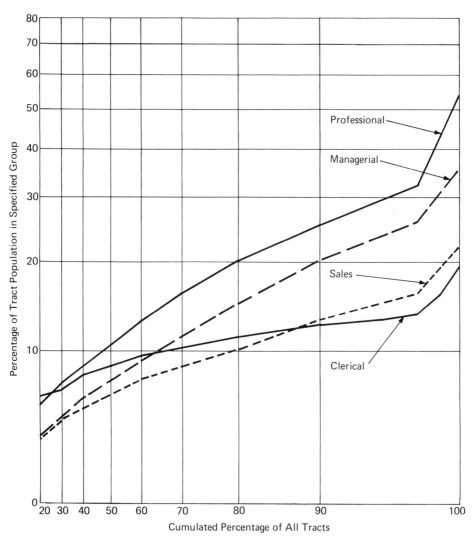

Figure 2-3. Segregation Curves for White-Collar Categories in the Boston SMSA, 1960.

is the greatest exception; aside from it, service workers, laborers, and professionals have the more remarkable concentrations at the curve's high end. But none of these look like the steeply rising curves for blacks, persons of Russian stock, or persons of Italian stock.

One last look at this kind of information will add another important conclusion. Figure 2-5 presents the segregation curves for blacks in the Boston SMSA from 1940 to 1960. It shows unmistakably that blacks were highly segregated over the entire period. It also shows that the pattern changed

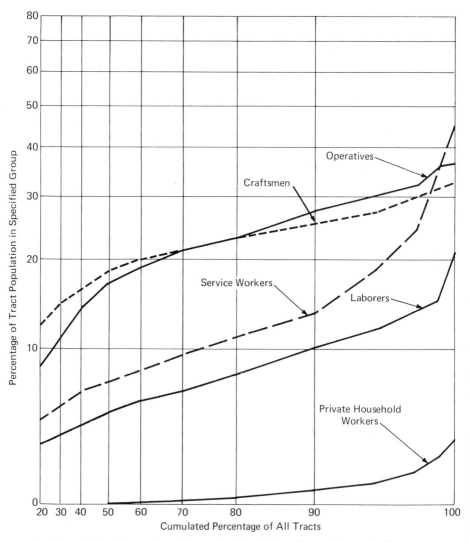

Figure 2-4. Segregation Curves for Blue-Collar Categories in the Boston SMSA, 1960.

somewhat as more blacks came and more whites left the central city. From 1940 to 1950 we see a definite increase in black segregation—the decisive formation of a ghetto. From 1950 to 1960 we find instead a consolidation of the ghetto; the differences between the two curves show basically the effects of increasing numbers rather than any important shift in the spatial pattern.

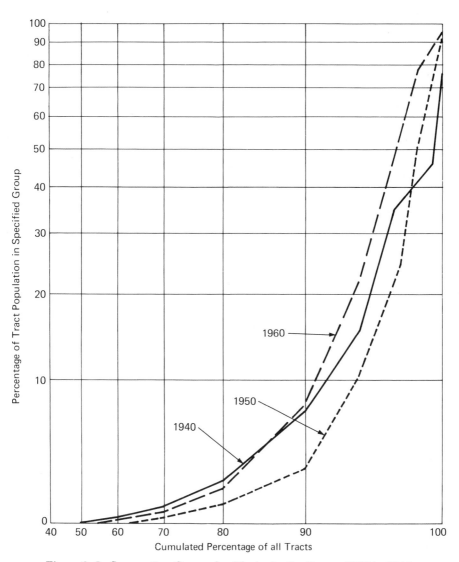

Figure 2-5. Segregation Curves for Blacks in the Boston SMSA, 1940–1960.

The Black Ghetto

From 1950 to 1960 the black population of the city of Boston increased by almost 60 percent. By 1960 more than half of the state's blacks lived in the city of Boston alone. The Boston suburbs (with triple the population of the central city) had only 14,000 blacks. In 1960, furthermore, 42,000 of the 63,000 blacks within the city lived in fourteen tracts in Roxbury, North Dorchester, and a corner of the South End. Figure 2-6 outlines and numbers the fourteen tracts. The jagged half-moon in Figure 2-7 forms Boston's ghetto.

The fourteen ghetto tracts contain some of Boston's largest clumps of rundown housing. Anyone who walks through them for awhile can get a reasonable idea: a few shady streets of substantial refurbished houses and apartments, a larger number of small, tidy one-family houses, grimy business streets backed by shabby gray tenements, block after block of disintegrating three-story apartments, stretches of rubble—so far unrenewed—interrupted and surrounded by sagging abandoned buildings and, once in awhile, a fresh new landscaped development of apartments and row houses. There is variety, and some good quality, in the ghetto's housing. But almost all of it is old. And even the passerby can tell that on the whole the ghetto dwellers are getting the worst of the housing market.

The 1960 census statistics on housing document the variety and the generally inferior condition of the homes in the ghetto. Our tables compare the fourteen ghetto tracts with the city as a whole. Table 2-3 lumps all the tracts together, so as to show more clearly how the ghetto's population—especially its black population—compares with the rest. In 1960 about 73 percent of these tracts' population, and about 9 percent of the city's population, was black: further-more, blacks comprised almost all (98.8 percent) of the nonwhites in the ghetto tracts, and over nine-tenths of the nonwhite population of the city as a whole. Table 2-3 shows three important things:

1. By comparison with the population of the entire city, on the average the nonwhite population had less education, moved more often, was more crowded, and occupied worse housing.
2. But the nonwhite population in the ghetto was remarkably similar in these respects to the nonwhite population outside.
3. And the whites and nonwhites living in the ghetto resembled each other greatly.

The only deviation from these generalizations that is large enough to pay much attention to is the higher proportion of nonwhites than of whites who had moved recently in the fourteen ghetto tracts.[c] That is due basically to the fact

---

[c]While the figures are for "total" and "nonwhite," one can easily deduce from these figures that 55 percent of the white households in the fourteen tracts were living in the same house as in 1955.

25

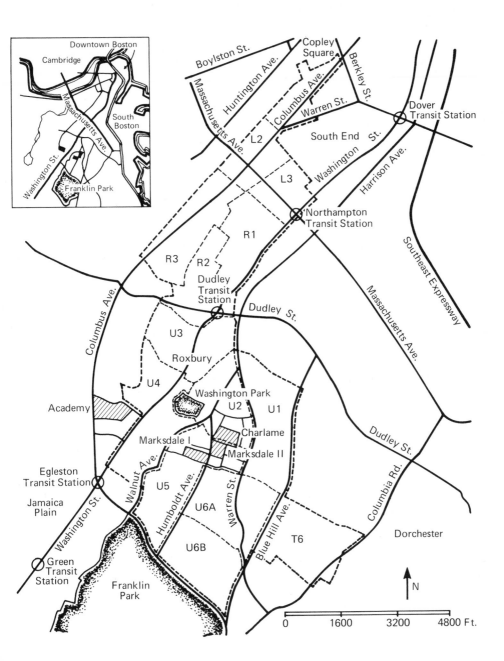

Figure 2-6. The Boston Ghetto: Some Approximate Boundaries.

26

that some of the areas in these predominantly black tracts had only recently opened up to black residents; in those sections the whites of 1960 were those who stayed, while the blacks were mainly newcomers.

When we look at individual tracts, as in Table 2-4, the considerable variety *within* the ghetto appears, but the main comparative conclusions remain. The income range goes from $2,750 in tract R-3 (an area of factories, railroads, truck routes, crowded side streets, boarded-up buildings, rubble, and a few patches of public housing) to more than double that in tract U-6B (an area of trim

Figure 2-7. Census Tracts in the City of Boston with 50 Percent or More Black Population, 1960.

Table 2-3

Selected Characteristics of Population and Housing in Predominantly Black Census Tracts in Boston, 1960

Item	Total Population		Nonwhite Population	
	14 Tracts	All Boston	14 Tracts	All Boston
Number of persons	57,745	697,197	42,503	68,493
Percentage Black	72.7	9.1	98.8	92.2
Percentage of population aged 25 or over high school graduates	34.4	44.6	36.6	36.2
Percentage living in same house in 1960 as in 1955	41.3	50.9	36.1	34.7
Percentage of occupied units owner occupied	15.8	25.6	16.0	15.7
Percentage of dwelling units deteriorating[a]	40.1	16.9	40.8	39.1
Percentage of occupied units dilapidated[a]	11.3	3.9	9.6	9.6
Percentage of households with 1.01 or more persons per room	9.7	7.5	11.5	13.2

[a]For total population, *all* dwelling units; for nonwhite population, *occupied* dwelling units.

apartments, single-family houses, and tree-shaded streets leading to a large park). The same two tracts stand lowest and highest in education. In each tract the income and education levels of nonwhite families are very similar to those of the total population. There is some tendency for the most nearly all-black tracts to rank low on education and income, and for those with little more than half the population black to rank high; the correlation is far from perfect. The amount of recent turnover depends partly on whether the buildings are mainly apartments, partly on how recently the area has opened up to blacks, partly on the impact of urban renewal. In the majority of the ghetto tracts, the white population has done less recent moving than the nonwhite. Again, the differences represent the fact that in many of these areas the white residents of 1960 were a remnant, the nonwhite residents a vanguard.

The same process operating in other cities shows up in Boston: a gradual movement of black families into areas of predominantly white population, mainly those adjacent to existing black settlements, with the blacks who move in generally similar or slightly superior to the resident population with respect to social and economic characteristics, and with the more prosperous and better-educated black families more likely to spearhead the movement. The process produces a good deal of segregation by class *within* the ghetto. It also means that the whites and nonwhites sharing any particular area resemble each other in

Table 2-4

Characteristics of Total and Nonwhite Population in Predominantly Black Census Tracts in Boston, 1960

Tract	Percentage Black	Median School Years Total	Median School Years Nonwhite	Median Family Income in 1959 (Dollars) Total	Median Family Income in 1959 (Dollars) Nonwhite	Percentage in Same House as in 1955 Total	Percentage in Same House as in 1955 Nonwhite
R-1	94.9	8.7	8.6	3178	3205	51.7	51.8
L-2	89.8	9.3	9.3	3804	3857	40.5	41.6
U-5	88.4	10.8	11.0	4927	5007	38.6	37.0
R-3	82.9	8.8	8.9	2750	2657	50.8	45.5
T-6	81.2	10.1	10.8	4239	4404	28.9	20.1
U-6A	81.0	10.4	10.8	5150	5195	40.9	35.4
U-2	77.7	9.6	9.6	4542	4228	37.5	31.1
L-3	71.1	8.9	9.4	3889	3750	45.9	39.3
U-1	63.5	9.9	10.8	5047	4771	45.7	37.2
J-2	59.1	10.7	10.8	3972	4085	50.5	56.8
U-4	57.7	10.1	10.8	5253	4652	45.5	33.9
R-2	54.4	8.9	8.5	3648	3549	47.0	42.2
U-6B	51.0	12.1	12.4	5518	5929	32.6	18.0
U-3	50.7	9.0	9.7	4533	4517	40.3	31.3
Boston City	9.1	11.2	10.2	5747	4235	50.9	34.7

many respects. Both of these phenomena stand out in the census data for Boston.

Finally, the statistics of housing in the individual tracts (Table 2-5) show less variety than the population characteristics do. In none of the tracts does the proportion of homeowners reach the average for the city as a whole. The proportion of units vacant and in the market stays in general at the high level of 5 to 7.5 percent. The "other vacant" figure is more erratic, most likely due to the vagaries of landtaking in urban renewal. With some exceptions, the proportion deteriorating or dilapidated fluctuates drearily between two-fifths and three-quarters of all dwellings. Except for two tracts containing large blocks of public housing, almost the entire housing stock is at least twenty years old. Yet the values of owner-occupied dwellings do vary, and roughly in correspondence with income. The rents vary less. The striking fact about them is that despite the deeply inferior condition of housing in these tracts, the rents run just about as high as elsewhere in the city. And in fact more detailed comparisons show that Boston blacks pay much more, and a much higher proportion of their income, for a given quality of housing than whites do. Boston shows the classic symptoms of the constricted, discriminatory housing market: blacks segregated, concentrated in old, rundown housing, paying more than the rent for comparable quality elsewhere in the city, ordinarily only leaving the ghetto by expanding it.

Table 2-5
Characteristics of Housing in Predominantly Black Tracts in Boston, 1960

Percentage of All Dwelling Units

Tract	Owner Occupied	Available Vacant	Other Vacant	Deteriorating	Dilapidated	Built Before 1946	Median Value Owner Occupied	Median Gross Rent Renter Occupied
R-1	7.7	7.1	11.6	41.1	17.8	79.9	5000	57
L-2	8.2	6.7	6.9	79.0	7.5	99.9	7900	64
U-5	17.3	4.0	1.9	25.8	6.7	98.9	11500	83
R-3	6.1	7.1	4.6	31.5	37.9	82.0	–	59
T-6	16.4	6.1	2.5	44.5	3.9	99.2	11600	80
U-6A	23.2	2.5	2.6	25.8	7.7	99.4	11000	86
U-2	19.0	7.2	4.9	29.6	12.5	98.7	7200	70
L-3	7.1	6.6	2.9	34.6	12.2	99.1	–	51
U-1	22.4	5.2	2.6	47.6	13.8	99.5	7700	78
J-2	11.1	7.5	1.8	54.8	2.1	100.0	7100	54
U-4	20.1	5.9	4.0	47.7	11.7	98.4	7900	78
R-2	13.8	6.5	19.1	35.7	31.9	98.1	5000	57
U-6B	10.4	3.9	0.6	10.0	0.8	100.0	16300	91
U-3	18.2	6.8	6.5	56.7	9.1	100.0	6400	66
Total These Tracts	14.1	5.8	4.6	40.1	11.3	96.9	–	–
Boston City	25.6	3.9	2.0	16.9	3.9	90.8	13500	78

A few blacks have found homes in the outer suburbs, especially the northwestern ones, since the mid-1950s. Their moves had great symbolic value, but their numbers were far too small to have a real effect on the general pattern of segregation. More blacks have moved into parts of North Dorchester and Jamaica Plain. But the main thing to happen has been the consolidation of the old ghetto. Since the 1950s various public actions have displaced many blacks but have not shaken segregation. While the whites who were displaced from the old West End, for example, scattered all over the metropolitan area, the blacks who were displaced from the South End moved practically en bloc to Roxbury and North Dorchester. Such a movement is doubly interesting. First, it shows the tenacity of racial segregation in Boston. Second, it illustrates the continuing importance of a sector reaching out south from the center of the city—with Washington Street and Blue Hill Avenue as major axes—as the main line of black expansion. The fact that the sector contains some of the highest-rent suburbs in the entire metropolitan area and the fact that the axis soon leaves the city of Boston suggest that new problems are on their way. Suburban school systems, suburban housing authorities, and suburban city officials will have to face decisions they have so far been content to leave to the central city.

The 1970 Census

While we have intentionally focused on 1960 census data in this chapter—since these figures depict the population and ghetto situation in Boston at the point in time closest to the beginning of the experimental rent subsidy program—available data from the 1970 census point up trends in Boston which persisted over the decade of the sixties. Between 1960 and 1970 the population of metropolitan Boston again increased, rising 6 percent, from 2,595,481 to 2,753,700.

Migration from other areas of the country continued to swell Boston's black population. Between 1960 and 1970 the metropolitan area's total black population also increased, rising from 78,000 to 127,000. Again over half of Massachusetts' total black population resided in the metropolitan Boston area. And, as was true for the previous decade, the central city of Boston absorbed most of this increase. In the central city the number of black urbanites increased from 63,000 to 105,000, while the number of white urbanites continued to decrease—by another 100,000. Thus the national pattern of black increase and white decrease in central cities of large metropolitan areas—in the case of Boston leading to a substantial rise in the proportion of the central city population which is black (from 9 percent to 16.3 percent) but only a slight increase in the black proportion for the metropolitan area (from 2.9 percent to 4.6 percent)—was characteristic of population trends in the Boston area in the 1960s as well as the 1950s. For the second decade in a row there was a decline in the total central city population of Boston. Although figures are not yet available on the points of origin of these new Bostonians, it appears that Boston is now receiving only a small share of the migrants following the traditional migration routes up the Atlantic coast.

In 1970 as in 1960 Boston's black population was still heavily concentrated in the South End, Roxbury, North Dorchester area (see Figure 2-6). Moreover, in 1970 the fourteen ghetto census tracts still included a very large percentage of the total black population in the central city. By 1970 the number of residents in those tracts had dropped somewhat, from 42,000 to 34,000, mainly as a result of urban renewal and related factors. While the proportion of the total black population in these particular tracts dropped from two-thirds to one-third, the proportion of the total black population in these tracts and in seven or eight *immediately contiguous* tracts to the west and southwest (particularly those in North Dorchester) was well over two-thirds in 1970. The gradual movement of black families into areas formerly white (mainly those adjacent to previous settlement areas) persists in the central city area.

Detailed socioeconomic characteristics are not yet available for the census tracts in the Boston ghetto area, so we cannot assess changes over time on such dimensions as income and education. However, we would expect no great surprises in these materials: some improvement but still a relatively deprived position of black Bostonions vis-á-vis the rest of Boston's population. Unfortunately, comparative statistics on such crucial housing characteristics as deterioration and dilapidation will never be available, since these factors were not measured in the 1970 census. The few general housing characteristics currently available indicate a significant rise in the vacancy rates (to more than 10 percent in most cases) and median contract rents for the fourteen central ghetto census tracts. In 1970, as in 1960, the overwhelming majority of the dwelling units in these tracts were renter-occupied. In general, then, these 1970 census data suggest a continuation of the trends of the fifties into the sixties.

Housing Trends in the Boston Area

After World War II the boom in Boston's science-based industries and the nationwide spurt of new suburban construction combined to rejuvenate the metropolitan area's housing stock. At first most of the new dwellings were single-family houses. But toward 1960 the balance shifted. In the five years after 1960, about half the dwellings constructed in the metropolitan area as a whole were apartments; in the city of Boston itself the proportion was closer to three-fourths. That does not mean people were becoming more crowded. In fact—in Boston, as elsewhere in the United States—people were breaking up into smaller households and demanding more space.

The net effect was a great increase in the quantity and the quality of the *metropolitan* housing stock. Even the central city gained in the 1950s, although more from thinning out, refurbishing, and scattered rebuilding than from massive new construction. Over the 1950s the city gained more than 6,000 dwelling units as it lost more than 100,000 people; that meant a drop from about 3.7 to about 3.1 persons per dwelling. The decade's changes also wiped out some of the substandard housing: 42,000 substandard units in 1950, 35,000 in 1960.

This process may have continued into the 1960s, although the data we secured from the Boston Redevelopment Authority and the City Building Department do not jibe very well with 1960 and 1970 census figures. Recently-released census reports indicate that the central city of Boston had only 232,448 housing units in 1970, compared to 238,802 in 1960—a *decrease* of 2.7 percent. However, for the period from 1960 to 1966 Boston Redevelopment Authority (BRA) figures indicate an apparent growth in dwelling units from about 238,000 in 1960 to 254,000 in 1966, a significant increase. We stress *apparent*, for two reasons: (1) the BRA "units added" in each year actually record building permits granted during that year rather than units completed and available for occupancy; one well-informed estimate is that at least 13,000 of the units for which permits were issued during the period remained to be completed and occupied at the end of 1966; this would reduce the true increase in the housing stock over the years 1960 to 1966; (2) some dwellings, like the houses long boarded up in wait for the construction of the Inner Belt or the renewal of Washington Park, disappear from the market some time before they disappear physically. As an FHA analyst put it:

The anomalous situation that exists with respect to a decline since 1960 in available rental units and an increase in unavailable vacancies results from the urban renewal taking place in the Central Submarket. Many tenants in areas programmed for renewal vacate voluntarily in anticipation of being displaced. In these areas, landlords often have difficulty in renting vacant units, and sometimes they withhold properties from the market because it is not economically feasible to make the long-range repairs or improvements necessary to make the units acceptable.[6]

While we cannot resolve the contradiction in the census, BRA, and FHA figures available to us, it is at least conceivable that the number of dwelling units in the city did increase in the early years of the decade (although much more slowly than BRA figures suggest) and then declined in the mid- and late-1960s.

Whether or not the number of housing units did increase in the early 1960s, we do know from the census data that density declined from 2.9 persons per housing unit in 1960 to 2.8 in 1970. Yet the costs and the benefits of housing trends were very unevenly spread. Those who paid the greatest personal costs rarely received substantial benefits. For example, the sample figures of the Boston Rental Housing Association indicate that by 1964 the practical *minimum* rent in the metropolitan area's modern apartments was around $120 per month.

By 1966, the FHA was reporting that "New apartments in Boston rent generally at $150 for efficiencies, $200-$240 for one-bedroom units, $225-$325 for two-bedroom units, and $350 and up for three-bedroom units."[7]

Even the lower figure of $120 demands an annual family income before taxes of at least $5,000.00—and of course the larger the family, the more rooms needed, the higher the rent, the less money left over for rent after food and clothing are paid for. Those figures mean that *virtually none* of the families in Boston's slums could afford to take direct advantage of new apartment construction.

Furthermore, vacancy statistics can be illusory. First of all, they vary widely by size of dwelling. The 1960 census yields estimates of proportions vacant (available and unavailable) of the following order.

Number of Bedrooms	Vacancy Rate
0	5.9%
1	6.3
2	8.8
3	7.0
4	2.4
5	2.4
6	2.7

These figures mean that finding a vacant apartment was much harder for the large households requiring four or more bedrooms. In addition, the massive renewal activity of the 1960s meant that an increasing proportion of "vacant" units was not actually available for rent; this was more true of the ghetto than of other parts of the city. Moreover, the 1967 FHA report on the Boston market indicates considerable fluctuation in the overall vacancy rate in rental units for the central area (Boston, Brookline, Cambridge, and Newton):

April 1960 (Census)	4.5%
April 1963 (postal survey)	2.6
July 1966 (postal survey)	2.8
October 1966 (FHA estimate)	3.2

In short, new apartment construction in Boston did not produce a notable surplus of dwellings for rent. Boston's low-income families did not benefit from it very much or very directly. With discrimination, uncertain employment, and even lower incomes than other people in Boston's rundown areas, that went double for blacks in the ghetto.

The alternative was "trickle down": families with enough money would move out of old but sound dwellings into new apartments, and poorer families from old, unsound dwellings would replace them. No doubt this often happened in

Boston. But there were several things wrong with the trickle. First, the new apartments were not built for the same sizes and shapes of families as already lived in the central city; for the most part, they were small and unsuitable for children. In fact, developers and city officials alike often hoped they would draw cosmopolitan adults into the city from elsewhere, rather than rehousing families already on hand. So it would take a great deal of heaving and hauling throughout the metropolitan market before the building of these high-rise apartments would ease the housing problems of large low-income families. Second, it maintained or increased the *gap* in housing quality between rich and poor, whites and blacks. The gains of blacks were trivial when compared with the gains of whites. Third, poor and black families bore the brunt of the tearing down which preceded the new building up. They were often shunted from house to house, they frequently found themselves living in half-destroyed neighborhoods, and they regularly ended up paying significantly more rent for only slightly better lodging.

To be sure, over the long run these changes may serve the poor families well. The massive renewal of Boston may eventually mean that everyone will be in better housing, and glad of it. Yet people live in the short run. To understand what the short run has been like, we should turn to look more directly at urban renewal in Boston.

Renewal in Boston

After decades of decline in the physical condition of the city and the beginning of decline in its population led to desultory experiments with clearance and rebuilding in the 1950s, Boston took up the task of renewal on a large scale around 1960. By that year major attempts at residential, commercial, or industrial reconstruction after extensive clearance were well underway in the New York Streets, Castle Square, and West End areas. After that, large residential renewal programs began in Washington Park and the South End. The completion of the vast, privately developed Prudential Center gave a new impetus to planning, and to the participation of private investors in Boston's development. The Government Center—the first of its kind in integrating city, state, and federal agencies in a single area—and the refurbishing of Boston's historic waterfront are examples of the scope of the Boston plan.

In a break with the plans of the 1950s, the General Neighborhood Renewal Plan issued in 1964 emphasized rehabilitation rather than clearance in Boston's rundown residential sections. The earlier plan, announced in 1952, had said:

Within the general framework of the over-all residential plan, most of the parts are fixed for many years to come. The vacant areas are subject to new planning. At the other end of the scale, slum areas are also subject to complete replanning as they are cleared for redevelopment. An important aspect of this plan is the determination of these development areas: the sections that require large-scale demolition in order to wipe out extremes of blight that levy severe social and economic costs upon the balance of the city.

Data, analyzed block by block, resulted in the marking out of areas so clearly substandard in building conditions and spacing that sweeping clearance of buildings is the only way they can be restored to social and economic health.[8]

In other words, tear down and start afresh. By the time the corresponding report of the plan proposed for 1965-1975 came out, the message was quite different:

The primary means of raising housing standards in Boston is rehabilitation. Through rehabilitation, the basic structural soundness of Boston's housing stock will be utilized without detracting from the City's other assets, particularly the unique, historical identity and cohesiveness of its individual communities. Urban Renewal remains the most effective method for rehabilitating housing on a large scale.[9]

To be sure, the improvement of the city's housing stock between 1952 and 1964 helps explain the shift in policy. Two other factors also played their parts: the rising outcry against large-scale clearance of residential areas, and the arrival in power of a redevelopment team with an expansive view of the scope of urban renewal.

The official plan sets up a housing target for the fifteen years from 1960 to 1975: 37,000 new units to be built, 32,000 more rehabilitated, against a probable 29,000 aging beyond recovery, for a net increase of 40,000 dwellings. Furthermore, less than a fifth of the new units are earmarked for low-income families (considered at the time of the proposal to be families with less than $4,000 per year). Some 15,000 of the 37,000 new units are supposed to be in moderate-income housing, and almost that many in high-rent, high-rise down-town apartments. Clearly the plan counts on abrupt reversals of two main trends in the population of Boston: the steady loss of people, the replacement of higher-income whites by lower-income blacks and whites. Indeed, the plan guardedly states such an intention:

Boston's population reached a peak of 801,000 in 1950 at a time when there was considerable over-crowding and considerably more substandard housing than there is today. Although in times past comprehensive plans for other cities have looked forward to significant gains in population, the policy of this Plan is that to do so here would encourage a more substantial commitment to high-rise housing construction than seems appropriate for Boston.

The Policy of the Development Program and this Plan is instead to promote stability in the size of Boston's population while increasing the diversity of its composition, so that it more nearly reflects the composition of the Region's population as a whole. This would, of course, entail a reversal of present trends toward increasing proportions of low-income groups and non-whites in the core City. However, this cannot be accomplished unless a positive effort is made to make residential Boston attractive to families at the time when they acquire the economic means to move elsewhere. For that reason, an important object of the Development Program must be to preserve the stability of residential neighborhoods in Boston and to make them, in as many respects as possible, competitive with surrounding cities and towns in housing, schools, and public services.[10]

The other side of this program, of course, is the movement of black and low-income families to the suburbs. It implies changes throughout the metropolitan area. It implies a new style of relocation. In these respects the plan is ambitious, controversial, and therefore politically explosive.

There are other reasons for its political impact. Over the planning period 1965-1975, Boston's General Plan requires the expenditure of billions of dollars, the construction of thousands of buildings, and the employment of a giant staff. The General Plan emphasizes regional development, an alien idea to many Boston politicians. The leadership of the Boston Redevelopment Authority has been in the hands of strong and vocal outsiders. Add to these facts the location of the major residential renewal projects of the mid-1960s in and around the black ghetto at the same time as segregation, discrimination, and civil rights have themselves become tense political issues in Boston; the result is a renewal program full of political tinder. The Redevelopment Authority has, in fact, often met opposition from those City Council members who conceive of government primarily in personal and local terms. And as the 1960s wore on, the conduct of urban renewal became an increasingly important point of contention in the city's election campaigns.

Geographically, the urban renewal program touches little of the city—mainly areas in or immediately around the central business district. But the use of these central areas strongly influences the pattern of activity elsewhere in the city. Furthermore, in recent years renewal has accounted for a large share of the changes in the city's total housing stock. Out of the approximately 12,000 dwellings destroyed in the city from 1960 through 1966, 7,500 were in areas undergoing renewal, and almost all of those directly attributable to the renewal program. So far, however, renewal has eliminated many more dwellings than it has produced.

Table 2-6 gives the details. Six years of vigorous renewal between 1960 and 1966 eliminated more than 7,500 dwellings from Boston's housing stock and added fewer than 4,500 in their place. The dwellings destroyed were, by and large, among the worst dwellings in the city, and they were, for the most part, occupied by families without much money. Most of the dwellings which replaced them, however, rented for much more than those which disappeared and were actually designed for different kinds of people. The best known case is the erection of the sleek, costly, cosmopolitan apartments of Charles River Park on the site once occupied by the drab three-deckers of the working-class West End. Castle Square offers a similar story in miniature. Even in Washington Park, the ghetto project, the net effect in the short run of 1960-1966 was to remove almost 2,500 dwellings occupied mainly by poor families and to build 800 dwellings devoted principally to families with incomes of $5,000 or more.

The chief renewal activity driving poor families into the housing market during the period of our study took place in Washington Park—the heart of the ghetto, in Lower Roxbury between Jamaica Plain and Dorchester. This 500-acre area housed about 25,000 people. While the Boston Redevelopment Authority's plan for the area relied much more heavily on rehabilitation than ever before, it still called for clearance of about 130 acres occupied by over 5,000 people. Up to the end of 1965 (when all the families in the rent subsidy experiment had moved into their new housing) 2,400 dwellings had been torn down. By that time only 460 new units were finished; they comprised the very three middle-income developments in which the forty families receiving rent subsidies found places. Of course, the longer-run plans included more low-income housing. In the meantime, the poor families had to wait.

Even within the ghetto, many of the better-off families seemed to accept or encourage the tendency of urban renewal to slight the poor. The *middle-income* black families in Washington Park, carefully studied by Watts and his associates in 1962 and 1963, at first seemed likely to leave the area entirely, in order to find better schools, quieter streets, more acceptable neighbors, and more

Table 2-6
Impact of Urban Renewal by Area, 1960-66

	Units Demolished	Units for Which Building Permits Issued in Period	Apparent Net Change	Additional Demolitions Planned	Additional New Units Planned	Net Change Planned
South End	150	500	+350	4950	3600	−1000
Jamaicaway	3	282	+279	0	0	+279
Prudential Center	0	542	+542	0	0	+542
Tremont-Mason	0	375	+375	0	0	+375
Washington Park	2453	789	−1664	0	711	−953
West End	3510	1440	−2070	0	960	−1110
Whitney Street	437	422	−15	0	148	+133
Government Center	989	0	−989	0	0	−989
Charlestown	0	0	0	675	1400	+725
Waterfront	0	0	0	0	1400	+1400
South Cove	0	0	0	281	600	+319
Fenway	0	0	0	810	3500	+2690
Total	7542	4350	−3192	6716	12319	+2411

Notes: Compiled from data supplied by the Research Division of the Boston Redevelopment Authority. The net figures substantially overestimate the units available for occupancy in these areas during 1960-66, since they make no allowance for the lag between the issuing of a building permit and the completion of the dwelling, or for the frequent lag between the razing of dwellings and the issuing of permits for new ones. For example, none of the 500 new South End units (more precisely, in Castle Square) was actually available at the end of 1966.

adequate shopping facilities—in short, a more middle-class environment.[11] (Judging from the tone of public and private discussions at the time, it is also quite possible that many of these people had the feeling that urban renewal would mean the shakeup of their own neighborhoods, the construction of massive public housing, and an influx of lower-class people.) But the Boston Redevelopment Authority's studious preservation of the middle-income neighborhoods, the emphasis on rehabilitation, the cutting out of plans for public housing, and the effective public relations device of "planning with people" via local organizations and open meetings allayed their anxieties. Almost *none* of the 250 families in the study actually moved out of the areas. A typical explanation came from a civil rights leader:

For the first two years we lived in Roxbury we were dissatisfied and looked forward to moving. We were particularly concerned because of the behavior of our Negro neighbors. Liquor bottles were thrown in the yard, there were fights every night in the apartments across the street and girls were raped in the neighborhood. It was not safe. But in the last two years we have thought less about moving from Roxbury. . . . There has been an improvement in the neighborhood. Most of the low-class Negroes have moved to Dorchester; those remaining seem to have more pride in the neighborhood. We don't find liquor bottles in our yard any more. A housing project for the elderly has been built nearby. As a result the neighborhood has been up-graded.[12]

That is, renewal had driven out undesirable neighbors and made the area more like those to which the middle-income families would otherwise have moved.

Morton Rubin's 1963 survey of a small cross-section of the Washington Park population brought out similar conclusions.[13] Rubin found that the low-income residents of Roxbury had not participated in the planning of renewal. Basically, clearance and rehabilitation alike bumped them into rundown, cheaper, adjacent neighborhoods.

Yet the New York Streets redevelopment project in the South End was held responsible for attracting some lower-class Negroes into Middle Roxbury. The spot-clearance features of the Washington Park Urban Rehabilitation project have caused fear on the part of low-income Negroes. It is the middle-class and the stable blue-collar worker groups that wish to rid the neighborhood of the lower-class group through renewal.

To this extent the neighborhood associations, church meetings, and the formal leadership represent the blue-collar small property owner and long-term tenant whose orientations to the middle class have succeeded through their children, who have been educated, have grown up, and have moved away. Stable blue-collar workers among these Negroes appreciate the need for adequate educational, recreational, and safety facilities in a rehabilitated neighborhood. They are not urban villagers. Their eye is on a future with civil rights rather than on the past. They are more like the generations of European migrants who preceded them to the city than they are like the present blue-collar remnant.[14]

In Rubin's view, this socially mobile segment saw its hopes fulfilled by urban renewal. Renewal flushed out the lower class. Segregation by class within the black community increased. And the middle class, real and would-be, stayed in place.

Relocation in Boston

By an unexpected turn, we have come back to relocation. The relocation required by urban renewal may be accelerating a double segregation of the central-city population: a separation of blacks from whites, a separation of classes within the black community. Both processes result from a combination of forces: a pattern of clearance which displaces the poorest people, and those with the least choice in the housing market, more often than the rest; the greater geographic range open to white families and wealthier ones when they *are* displaced; deliberate restriction and concentration of the housing available to poor black families. Other forces like new housing legislation and the loosening of the central-city housing market are working in the other direction, toward the residential integration of the central city.[15] The net effect is little change in the extent of segregation within the central city, but a steady increase of segregation at the metropolitan scale.

We do not yet have enough solid evidence to say that the overall effect of relocation from the Washington Park renewal sites has been to sort out the black population by class. That seems likely. Since the official relocation reports do not distinguish race or income (and in any case miss a significant proportion of the families actually displaced), they do not provide the necessary information. Yet even they make it clear that the relocation experience of blacks from Washington Park has differed fundamentally from that of the whites moved out of the West End. In the case of the West End:

... the most striking feature of the redistribution is its "shotgun" pattern ... , the absence of large-scale clustering in the vicinity of the project area, the relatively weak centripetal pull within a six mile radius of the West End, and the spread of large numbers of families into virtually every section of Boston and every one of the inner core suburbs. Approximately the same number of relocated families are found in each of the first five mile rings surrounding the West End. 38% relocated outside Boston in other parts of the metropolitan area, and another 6% left the metropolitan area entirely.[16]

But for the 1,580 relocated Washington Park families reported on early in 1966, the new residences were located as follows:

Washington Park	24.6%
Other Roxbury	25.1
Dorchester	25.4
Jamaica Plain	7.0
Other	13.8
Unknown	4.1
	100.0%

More (probably much more) than 80 percent of the families, in other words, moved within two miles of their previous dwellings.[17] This means that most of them relocated *within the ghetto*. If we could separate the whites on the list from the blacks, the chances are that they would account for most of the movers outside of Roxbury and Dorchester. Even in the absence of the crucial information, it is hard to escape the impression that relocation from Washington Park either displaced or consolidated the ghetto.

Why and how? The main factors are well known: discrimination in the housing market, reluctance of many blacks to leave the black community, limits set by places of work, poverty, reliance on local, casual, and personal ways of finding housing. The difficulty is to assign them weights and to understand their interdependence. Watts and his associates, in their analysis of Washington Park families, concluded that the more prosperous black families could buy satisfactory housing in predominantly white suburbs if they wanted to, but that a variety of anxieties, commitments, and local satisfactions kept most of them close to the ghetto; they ended up arguing for an attack on discrimination in the downtown rental market and the attraction of whites into the ghetto.[18] But to the extent that blacks are segregated, they are vulnerable to discrimination in both the cost and the quality of the housing they receive. The sharp distinction of "Negro" from "white" areas—an asymmetrical distinction in practice, since there are almost always some whites in "Negro" areas but not vice versa—reduces the black's choice, bargaining power, and value received. Under present conditions, prosperous blacks who choose to remain in the ghetto compound the problems of those who have no choice.

Public policy has a nettle to grab. Providing sound housing, advancing integration, and following the desires of black families contradict each other (although not totally, and perhaps only in the short run). Which comes first? By and large, public authorities have opted for sound housing, even if they have not succeeded in getting it.

Public Housing

Public housing illustrates the prickly nature of the problem. From 1935 to 1955, the city of Boston built a good deal of conventional low-rent public housing. In the latter year the Boston Housing Authority opened up the largest of its big developments, Columbia Point. By that time it had 14,000 apartment units. Between 1955 and 1970 the BHA added only a few hundred apartments mainly in small developments designed for old people.

By the mid-1960s, the 14,000 apartments were virtually fully occupied, turnover was less than 2,000 per year, some 4,000 new applications were coming in each year, and there were 8,000 to 9,000 families on the waiting list.[d] The

---

[d]These figures, taken from official BHA documents, are higher than commonly quoted statistics, but jibe with our own analyses of the waiting lists.

squeeze on the smallest and the largest apartments was enormous; at the rates of turnover prevailing then, it would have taken more than twelve years to find a place for every eligible applicant for a one-bedroom apartment, and almost as long to house every applicant requiring an apartment of five bedrooms or more. This meant that the displaced families the Redevelopment Authority hoped to lodge in public housing would face stiff competition. No doubt that is one reason the BRA's plan called for the construction of at least 5,000 new units of public housing.

The same desire to get rid of the lower class which seems to activate some of the enthusiasm for renewal in Washington Park may frustrate the BRA's hopes to put some of the 5,000 public housing units there. At the end of April 1966 the people at a neighborhood meeting in the Seaver-Townsend area of Washington Park voted against a BRA-BHA proposal to build a 30-unit development there; faithful to "planning with people," the BRA then dropped the proposal.[19] BRA director Edward Logue ruefully commented: "While I think the community decision was a mistake, I think it is a decision which should be respected. . . . " The account in the *Boston Globe* pointed out that the opponents of public housing were only 45 out of the 200 reported to have attended the meeting, and out of the 15,000 people in the Seaver-Townsend section. The *Globe's* reporter went on to some interesting observations:

Logue's response has some validity since the group involved in the renewal planning process, the Washington Park Urban Renewal Action Committee, has worked hard the past three years for the renewal improvements.

Without its cooperation, a renewal program never could have gotten off the ground. But some observers think Logue's quick acceptance of the vote is shrugging off the city's responsibility for housing low-income families adequately. They point out that in order to make the improvements the middle-class community wanted, dilapidated housing occupied by low-income groups had to be demolished.

. . .

Advanced were arguments that public housing would further ghettoize the area. Clergy took the opposite view, but in vain.

State Rep. Michael Haynes made a salient point that it was the inarticulate masses who needed public housing who were not at the meeting to vote.

Again the middle-class residents of Washington Park seem to have used their superior organizational skills to shape urban renewal. The irony is that in proposing a development as small as 30 units, the BRA and BHA were making a sharp break with previous practice and undertaking an experiment which could combat segregation.

Boston's existing public housing stands in large, segregated blocks. Except for the units designed specifically for the elderly, the developments average around 550 apartments each. The range goes from an exceptionally small 72 (Camden Street, Roxbury) to a bulky 1,504 (Columbia Point). By design, they are segregated in terms of income. In fact, they are also segregated in terms of color.

For the most part, the developments in the ghetto have extraordinary proportions of blacks, the developments outside very few. The big variations follow the racial patterns of the city as a whole. But within those big variations are some striking and worrisome exceptions.

The pattern of segregation, and the complaint that the Boston Housing Authority's tenant selection procedures worked against blacks, made admission into public housing in Boston a civil rights issue in the 1960s. In 1962 the Boston chapter of the NAACP brought a complaint against the Housing Authority before the Massachusetts Commission Against Discrimination (MCAD). In 1963, the MCAD, CORE, NAACP, and the Housing Authority reached an agreement placing the responsibility for racially integrated public housing with the Housing Authority's administrators. The administrators were offered the help of concerned community leaders.

Public housing survey statistics issued by the MCAD indicated that the Housing Authority did increase the total number of black residents in public housing from 2,058 in 1962 to 3,163 in 1965.[20] By that time blacks had found places in every development except two small, outlying projects for the elderly. Yet the basic pattern remained. The most striking example appeared in two developments located across the street from each other: Mission Hill and Mission Hill Extension. The figures for numbers of black families were:

Development	Number of Units	1962	1963	1964	1965
Mission Hill	1,023	1	3	21	42
M.H. Extension	588	504	518	531	524

This pattern continued into the late 1960s. In Boston as elsewhere, the current rate of change could not produce desegregated public housing for a long time to come.

What were the housing officials to do? Few apartments opened up each year, white applicants (often for legitimate reasons) generally preferred developments outside the ghetto, black applicants (often for legitimate reasons) frequently preferred developments in or near the ghetto, and practically no one wanted to shuffle the families already established in public housing. They revamped their selection and assignment procedures and made it harder for a family to refuse an apartment on racial grounds. But it would obviously be much easier for them to foster integration if new public housing in small blocks and on well-chosen sites went up, and if there were attractive alternatives to public housing for low-income families.

By the late 1960s public housing tenant groups had formed and pressed the Housing Authority to improve the safety and sanitary conditions of existing projects. The ensuing litigation suggests that the formation of such tenant groups might conceivably speed the pace of change in public housing, not just in regard to environmental conditions but in regard to segregation and building practices as well.

Other Programs.

Some of the alternatives being tried in Boston operate within the existing housing stock, while others affect the stock itself. In the first category are the aid in dealing with landlords offered by Call for Action, the house-finding efforts of Fair Housing Incorporated (FHI), and the housing complaint procedures of the Massachusetts Commission Against Discrimination. In the second are a few private efforts at low-cost residential rehabilitation, the Boston Housing Authority's leasing program, and the BHA combination of 221 (d) (3) construction with direct rent subsidies.

Call for Action, administered by the American Friends Service Committee, operated from a Roxbury storefront. Through radio spot announcements, and other means, it solicited telephoned complaints about housing conditions. In 1965 the organization received complaints worth recording from about 400 families. In most of these cases a Call for Action worker went to the dwelling, checked out the complaint, spotted other housing defects, then talked with the landlord about his responsibilities. If that did not solve the problem, the worker usually went to one of a variety of agencies—the Health Department, the Housing Inspection Department, and so on. Our analysis of the records of 376 families served by Call for Action in 1965 and early 1966 indicates that roughly a quarter of the families ended up with their complaints definitely satisfied, a quarter got mixed results, a quarter finished by moving out, and a quarter received no satisfaction at all. Our analysis also suggests that even in this agency dealing mainly with poor families and miserable housing, the smaller families paying more rent (probably the higher-status families) are more likely to see their problems solved. This appears to be due partly to the fact that they live in sounder housing in the first place, and partly to the greater readiness of their landlords to act.

The advantage of the higher-status black family shows up even more clearly in the operation of Fair Housing Incorporated. The establishment of FHI in 1963 stepped up and formalized the metropolitan Fair Housing Federation's operation of a clearing house helping blacks to find dwellings in predominantly white sections of the metropolitan area. With the aid of a federal grant the organization undertook to serve more low-income families than the federation's volunteer efforts had been able to. Three hundred to 400 people per year applied to FHI. An evaluation of the program by the Joint Center for Urban Studies showed, unsurprisingly, that the great majority of the people who found places to live in integrated areas with FHI's help were middle class in income, occupation, and outlook.[21] Even the lower-income persons tended to be couples or single individuals in the early stages of white-collar careers. Furthermore, the lower-income people who did apply to FHI less often found housing in predominantly white residential neighborhoods; among those who found any housing at all, the proportion going to such neighborhoods was around 40 percent for low-income applicants (the other 60 percent going into public housing, segregated neighborhoods, or neighborhoods well on their way to segregation) and over 70 percent for those with higher income. In this case, the criterion for "low income" was rather generous, since it was the amount of income a household could have and yet remain in public housing. Out of the 219 applicants who found housing in integrated areas over a two-year period, only 22 reported annual incomes of less than $4,000. Of them, closer inspection showed the following breakdown:

Single student or white-collar worker	6
Other single person	4
Larger white-collar or student household	2
Other household of two persons or more	9

Furthermore, six of the nine "other households" ended in public housing. All in all, FHI's connections with a large network of suburban organizations permitted it to ease the movement of middle-class blacks to the suburbs. But its usual procedures could hardly help poor families of any size.

Fair Housing Incorporated did set up one other crucial service: testing discrimination in the housing market. Anyone who suspected he had been refused housing on racial grounds could go to the agency, which would ordinarily send out a white tester representing himself as having similar housing needs and resources. Sometimes the case would then be settled informally, but often the next step was a complaint before the Massachusetts Commission Against Discrimination. In 1963 Massachusetts enacted the most extensive fair housing law in the country and made the MCAD one of its chief agents. During 1964 and 1965 FHI helped initiate more than two-thirds of all the housing complaints which came to the commission.

The MCAD itself has been active in investigating such complaints. It has made a significant contribution in the protection of the legal rights of persons who have experienced clear-cut discrimination. Furthermore, the commission annually reviews the tenant selection policies of the public housing authorities of Massachusetts and the published statistics on nonwhite families in public housing. Yet its impact on the housing market is indirect and long-run. In 1965, for example, the MCAD received 134 housing complaints. Thirty-one people who brought complaints then or in the previous year got the dwellings they had at first been refused, or comparable units; another thirty-three were offered such dwellings but turned them down—commonly because they had moved somewhere else long since.[22] However, as a result of the actions of MCAD and FHI in the area of housing discrimination, together with the correlative strengthening of fair housing laws, by the late 1960s it had at least become possible for black Bostonians with adequate financial resources to secure housing in suburban areas.

Boston's three largest organized efforts in the mid-1960s to help blacks get decent housing within the existing market, then, have several features in common: small numbers of applicants relative to the large numbers in bad housing, low rates of clear-cut success, much greater success with higher-income families than with others. This combination of characteristics makes it seem unlikely that simply by expanding the efforts would it be possible to significantly improve the housing or decrease the segregation of Boston's low-income blacks. Indeed, these problems perhaps explain in part the demise of both Call for Action and Fair Housing Incorporated a few years later. New organizations, such as the Association for Better Housing, Inc. (ABH) and the Roxbury Action Program, did emerge in the late 1960s as partial replacements for the defunct groups. In 1967 ABH, a nonprofit social service agency, was set up to aid low- and moderate-income families to buy homes in the Boston area. Yet, so far as we have been able to discern, the problems of relatively small numbers served and greater success with families above the poverty line continue to suggest that as Boston moves into the 1970s such private programs will not make a great dent in Boston's low-income housing problem.

That leaves the alternatives of putting more coercion into such efforts, intervening more directly in the market by manipulating prices and incomes, or changing the housing supply itself. Nineteen sixty-six housing legislation in Massachusetts did strengthen the tenant's hand vis à vis the landlord by giving the tenant the possibility of paying his rent into an escrow fund, when the landlord is not keeping the dwelling up to standard, and by making eviction more difficult. There are also recurrent ritual attempts to stiffen housing inspection. However, the most promising programs tried so far have combined intervention in the market with changes in the housing supply.

Urban renewal, of course, includes massive intervention of that kind. We have seen that the immediate net effect of renewal on the segregation and quality of housing occupied by poor black families in Boston has been, at best, to produce more of the same at the cost of considerable pushing around, at worst, to consolidate the ghetto, raise rents, and give the families less choice. Other programs—generally received with enthusiasm by the Boston Redevelopment Authority, it must be said—have sought to counteract those effects. Several private organizations, typified by the Roxbury Development Corporation, have tried to promote the investment of capital in ghetto housing, the rehabilitation of the housing, sale or rental at a reasonable price, and the provision of neighborhood facilities. At least from the outside, these enterprises seem to have been successful on a very small scale.

In addition to the rent subsidy experiment, the Boston Housing Authority began two other public interventions in the housing market in the mid-1960s, one small and one large. The small program was to consist of acquiring just over a hundred units of old but sound housing, renovating them, and operating them as public housing. May Hipshman describes that experiment as follows:

In 1964, the BHA purchased some 40 units of row housing in the Highland Park section of Roxbury, planning to rehabilitate them for large-family occupancy. An architect of considerable local reputation (who had, however, no previous experience with rehabilitation) was hired, but even after he had revised his plans several times, estimates far exceeded HAA cost ceilings. Reports are that estimated costs per unit, including acquisition and rehabilitation, approached $28,000. The high cost was partly due to the fact that the buildings had to be gutted almost entirely, in order to combine small apartments into larger ones, and also because local building codes and HAA requirements called for certain room sizes, hall widths and other standards which were difficult to apply in structures as old as these. The buildings stood vacant for nearly two years; vandals did considerable damage, and a fire did more. The buildings have now been demolished.[23]

And the program was shelved.

The large program was related to the new Section 23 Leasing Program and was at first to consist of leasing 1,000 scattered standard units—some new, some recently rehabilitated, and some old but sound. Since the maintenance of the property remains the owner's responsibility, and the tenant pays rent to the Housing Authority at normal public housing rates while the Authority pays the full negotiated rent to the owner, the leasing program resembles the use of direct rent subsidies as in the experiment. The biggest difference is that it can not add new housing. By mid-1967 the authority had leased about 70 units. By mid-1968 it had almost 500 units. And by the early 1970s only 2000 units were occupied. The BHA encountered quite a bit of difficulty in bringing privately owned dwellings into the program. More important, the Leased Housing Department of BHA was understaffed and had suffered through many administrative problems. If this program continues to develop, nevertheless, it offers an important promise of sound housing and economic integration at the same time.

That brings us back to Boston's experimental rent subsidy program. With the 1965 Housing and Urban Development Act, a program quite similar to the Boston experiment—titled the Rent Supplement Program—was formally inaugurated. But when the Boston Housing Authority began planning for its pioneering program in the early 1960s, the idea of subsidizing the rent of poor Americans in private housing was still quite experimental—and extremely controversial. Why the rent subsidy approach to housing the poor has been so *hotly debated and condemned* will become clearer if we digress for a moment to sketch some of the background to national policy on rent subsidies, particularly developments leading to and surrounding the enactment of the 1965 Rent Supplement legislation.

3

Political Controversy Over Rent Subsidies: The Emergence of the Rent Supplements Program

Introduction

In the mid-1960s the proposed use of direct rent subsidies in the private market as an aid to the rehousing of poor families not only suggested a promising alternative to existing public policy but also offered a new opportunity to learn something about the divergent perspectives on housing policy present in the United States. Many saw the new proposals as bold, innovative, and even revolutionary. Others saw rent subsidies as highly suspect, perhaps even as un-American and socialistic. Whatever one's assessment, the idea of subsidizing rents—at least in the form of directly paying to a private landlord the difference between what a poor family could afford to spend on housing and the economic rent of a sound dwelling acceptable to them—was seen as highly provocative and quite unconventional.

Not that the idea of the rent subsidization was really brand new. In the United States the idea of subsidizing the housing of the poor has been debated vigorously but inconclusively for over thirty years. And the idea follows quite reasonably from an even older awareness of the bad fit between the operation of the private market and the needs of poor families. Nearly a century ago Frederick Engels published a monograph, "The Housing Question," which dealt with the growing and rather serious housing problems of the European working classes. As one might expect, Engels chided the capitalist philanthropists for their naiveté in believing that private capital would ever be willing to fund a large amount of low-income housing—and a large amount of such housing was desperately needed. A similar belief has set the tone of much of the debate over housing legislation of the last thirty years. Thus proponents of low-rent public housing in the 1930s and 1940s argued very persuasively that the private housing industry in the United States had shown itself incapable of providing standard housing for large numbers of low-income families. Indeed, in the 1930s no less a conservative than the late Senator Robert A. Taft defended the public housing program on this very basis. In contrast to most Republicans in the debate over the housing legislation of the 1960s he argued strongly for a bill which provides federal subsidization "for those unable to pay an adequate rent." Yet, quite predictably, some business opponents of the proposed low-rent public housing legislation saw it as a socialistic invasion of an area previously dominated by private enterprise and would have nothing to do with it.

However, during the debates of the 1930s yet other business and housing industry opponents took a quite different tack. They proposed an alternative plan similar in many ways to the Boston experimental program and the Rent Supplements Program eventually included by the administration in the 1965 Housing Act. Although severely criticized by many Republicans and other conservatives during the 1960s, the direct rent subsidy idea was—over thirty years ago—partially forged in their own furnaces and propagated by many of their own representatives. Although the plans sometimes varied in detail and the terms used varied somewhat, the general idea was the same: to give the private market the chance to house low-income families by providing a government-financed direct rent grant to each needy family which would be adjusted to its income. But the protagonists in the debate changed between the 1930s and the 1960s—perhaps most clearly seen in the debates over the 1965 housing legislation.

Some Early Experiments

In a quiet way, and on a small scale, the Housing and Home Finance Agency had been encouraging trials of the direct rent subsidy principle for several years before the 1965 housing legislation debates captured the attention of the mass media. Here we pause briefly to give the reader some capsule descriptions of some important programs—other than the Boston housing experiment—as they were operating early in 1966:

Chicago. Rent assistance to elderly low-income families takes the form of monthly payments from the housing authority to the management of private apartments to make up the difference between rent low-income elderly families can afford and the full amount of the rent. About 100 families are involved. The housing authority inspects the buildings and negotiates rentals.

San Francisco. The city's experimental assistance program is confined to cooperative and condominium housing. The State Department Fund subsidizes the rents of sixty low-income families displaced from urban renewal sites whose prospects for increasing their incomes looks promising. The families are interspersed, without distinction, among middle-income families in three different cooperative or condominium housing developments in renewal areas.

St. Louis. The St. Louis County Development Authority is subsidizing the rents of twenty low-income families displaced by urban renewal. They occupy twenty of fifty units in newly-constructed middle-income dwellings in the same renewal area. The authority issues a monthly rent assistance check made out jointly to the family and the landlord. The tenant endorses the check, adds to it his monthly payment, and turns it over to the landlord. The amount of the check varies according to family income.

New Haven. The Housing Authority subsidizes the rents of low-income families of seven persons or more in standard privately owned and managed apartments, under lease between private management and the tenants. Prior to the signing of the leases, the Authority negotiated fair rents case-by-case, with the tenant paying one-fifth of his income as rental and the Authority making up the difference with a "rent assistance" check paid directly to the management. Forty families were to benefit from the program, but as of this report fewer than thirty were in it, due to the difficulty of finding suitable apartments.

In addition to these federally assisted programs, a few states had launched their own rent subsidy arrangements in the mid-1960s. The programs in action up to that point in time varied in the housing they dealt with, in the sorts of low-income families involved, and in the mechanics of the subsidy.

The 1965 Housing Legislation and its Aftermath

While a few rent subsidy experiments, quietly sponsored by the Housing and Home Finance Agency, were well underway by 1965, a fierce and sometimes bitter controversy began to rage across the country over the supposedly "new" rent subsidy program proposed in 1965 by President Lyndon Johnson. In March 1965 President Johnson forwarded his message dealing with urban problems to Congress, a message emphasizing what he considered to be a new program of rent supplements for low- and moderate-income families who were displaced by urban renewal, elderly, handicapped, or living in substandard housing.[1] The initial request proposed a housing program including moderate-income families who fell into these various categories. In the words of the message, such an approach would provide new flexibility which "will allow us to help people across a much broader range of income than has hitherto been possible." The president emphasized that this "most crucial new instrument" in our effort to improve our cities would involve private builders and would provide housing for both low- and moderate-income families.

As might have been expected, the controversy over directly subsidizing the rents of American families was especially vigorous in Washington, D.C. "FHA for the poor," "renticare," "residential socialism," "Brook Farm Act of 1965," "disaster relief program"—the phrasemakers had a field day with the new Rent Supplements Program. Indeed, the Rent Supplements Program has been one of the most talked about, and perhaps least understood, housing proposals in the recent history of the American Congress. Moreover, the arguments in the congressional debates over the Rent Supplements Provision of the 1965 Housing Act were rather typical of housing arguments over subsidies before and since. Of course, those engaged in the congressional debates did not realize just how typical the issues they raised would become in subsequent controversies over, and evaluations of, a variety of rent subsidy proposals. But many of the issues were basic:

1. Should this housing program focus on low- or moderate-income families, or both?
2. Should families displaced by public action be included?
3. What levels of income and assets should determine who is eligible?
4. What types (old, new, profit, nonprofit) private housing should be included?
5. Would the program be more costly than the traditional public housing approach?
6. Would economic "haves" and "have nots" be forced to mix, to integrate residentially? Would this create intergroup hostility?
7. Would the program foster racial integration or segregation in private housing?
8. Should the location of the subsidized housing units be locally controlled?
9. Would the role of private business in such a program be central?
10. Would the program destroy the achievement incentive of poor Americans? Where does the proposal stand in light of traditional free enterprise philosophies?

Since a number of these issues and questions are directly relevant to our evaluation study of Boston's experimental housing program—indeed, we can shed some light on certain of these crucial questions—and are critical to understanding public policy in the housing area, we will here digress a bit to look closely at the turbulent history of the Rent Supplements Program.

House Subcommittee Hearings

Within a month of the president's message the Housing Subcommittee of the House of Representatives began hearings on an omnibus housing bill (H.R. 5840) including the president's Rent Supplements Provision (Title 1, Section 101). In this early stage HHFA Administrator Weaver stressed, in testimony before the Housing Subcommittee, that the program would aid *middle-income* families, those with incomes too high for public housing and too low for private home ownership.[2] In reply to a question about the great need for housing *low-income* families, Weaver replied that the government was trying to meet that particular need through public housing. The government rent supplement would make up the difference between 20 percent of an occupant's income and his market rent. At the outset administration officials took full advantage of the propaganda possibilities inherent in the proposal by pointing up the largely private nature of the program: federal money would go to owners of housing built for private profit, and would be paid directly to owners and subject to their tenant selection procedures ("private enterprise"). Actually the final form of the bill limited payments to what might be termed "quasi-private" housing, that is, only to housing built by cooperatives, limited-dividend corporations, or nonprofit associations.

Albeit in rudimentary form, several arguments against this plan of government rent subsidization appeared during these House hearings on the program, foreshadowing those in subsequent debates. One major issue which arose was that of income ceilings and asset limits for persons admitted to the program.[3] Much criticism of the program focussed on what were considered to be excessively high income ceilings. This issue was to come up again and again. In fact, this issue alone was to kill the program for a time, until it was resolved by new HHFA guidelines issued in December 1965. Another criticism of the program as initially designed concerned its focus on families above the lowest and—as several spokesmen pointed out—the most needy income level. This provision of an income "floor" was later altered by the House Banking and Currency Committee to include the lowest income level.

Anticipating heated discussion in House floor debates to come, one worried New York congressman asked HHFA Administrator Weaver if he intended to use the Rent Supplements Program to promote integration other than income integration. Weaver was vague and noncommittal.[4] Although this issue of racial integration was barely touched on in the hearings, it would later surface in more virulent form. Moreover, some testimony during the hearings, such as that of the spokesman for the National Conference of Catholic Charities, welcomed the prospect of economic integration and cited the therapeutic value of integrating low-income families with so-called normal families.[5]

During these hearings several industry organizations, such as the National Association of Home Builders, supported the Rent Supplements Program but objected to its conception as a substitute for the older 221 (d) (3) program, which they saw as a workable program for housing moderate-income families.[6]

One of the strongest arguments against the "new" rent supplements approach was presented during these House hearings by the president of the National Association of Housing and Redevelopment Officials (NAHRO), an organization whose members had a vested interest in public housing.[7] He argued that this "new" program was "administratively cumbersome and socially undefensible." As he saw it, the traditional public housing approach was actually a cheaper way for the federal government to provide the housing that was needed. It was also pointed out that local housing authorities, having had great experience in this area, could do a much better job than private nonprofit agencies in administering such programs.

One other criticism of the original program arising in the hearings was that it was too self-limiting, that it covered only new housing and applied only to nonprofit organizations. In testimony during the hearings several industrial and civic spokesmen argued that the program should also cover rehabilitated housing and housing built by "profit" organizations. (Rehabilitated housing was soon to be included in the bill, but unlimited "profit" sponsors were not.)

During the hearings opponents of the Rent Supplements Program in its original form included the National Association of Real Estate Boards, the National Association of Housing and Redevelopment Officials, and the National Lumber and Building Materials Association; the U.S. Chamber of Commerce spokesman hinted that the chamber would prefer other approaches to the administration's rent supplements approach. Organizational supporters of supplements included the AFL-CIO, the National Association of Home Builders, the Mortgage Bankers Association, the National Conference of Catholic Charities, the National Council on Aging, and the National Association of Mutual Savings Banks, although several of these groups qualified their endorsement. Interestingly, private-enterprise-oriented organizations could be found on both sides of the issue.

The House Banking and Currency Committee voted out the Housing and Urban Development bill in the late spring of 1965, with the rent supplements section substantially modified to cover persons who could not find standard housing at rents up to 25 percent of their current incomes (rather than the original 20 percent) *and who were eligible for public housing.* For the first time this latter addition specifically made low-income families eligible for supplements, the very families who had been excluded under the original administration proposal.[8] However, like the original proposal this version limited supplements to persons who were aged, disabled, displaced by government action, or currently occupying substandard housing. At this point in its trajectory through the Congress the bill authorized $50 million for the first fiscal year (1966); the figure was to reach $200 million in fiscal 1969.

The Republican opponents on the House Banking and Currency Committee filed a minority report on the rent supplements section of the bill, which they circulated at their own expense. Since many of the arguments heard in and out of Congress from 1965 to 1969 echo the arguments made in this document, they are worth discussing in some detail.[9] The first argument of these opponents asserted that the supplements formula "kills the incentive of the American family to improve its living accommodations by its own efforts." By this they meant that a family with a $250-a-month income could live in a $100-a-month apartment with the federal subsidy; if its family income increased, the subsidy would then be reduced. "It can live in the same accommodations with a $250 a month income as it could if it increased its income to $400 a month." They argued that subsidizing a family's rent would obviously kill its incentive to raise its income or, for that matter, to own a home.

A second worry expressed in the minority report related to what were seen as rather high income limits in the bill, an issue that had been raised during the earlier House hearings. It was calculated that "upper-middle-income" families could qualify for rent supplements, especially if the HHFA administrator chose to ignore secondary sources of income. In addition, they made the assertion that, because the administrator is bound only by high dollar limits per unit under FHA mortgage insurance programs, a supplements family could conceivably be moved into a penthouse costing $100,000. "The occupant could be a large family eligible for rent supplements, with its entire income derived solely from public assistance payments." Among other things this argument assumed that the administrator would not count public assistance payments in calculating the rent limits for such a family. This extremely exaggerated view that the supplements program would enable the poor to live in government-subsidized penthouses persisted, surprisingly enough, into later debates. It gave an early sign that the debates were polarizing along ideological lines.

Another major fear was "economic integration." The Rent Supplements Program would mean across-the-board economic integration, enabling a poor man ("economic lambs") to live in neighborhoods with the rich ("economic lions"). This argument apparently had undertones of fear of racial integration, a fear which had briefly surfaced in earlier House hearings and would manifest itself much more explicitly in later House and Senate floor debates.

A fourth argument made by these opponents was that the program would jeopardize the traditional public housing program. According to their estimates the cost per unit could be much higher under the Rent Supplements Program than under the older public housing program. This argument too appears again and again in the 1965-69 discussions, and proponents of rent supplements found it necessary to counterattack with per unit statistics. A fifth major argument expressed in the minority report was the general assertion that rent supplements were "the way of the socialist state." The specter of socialism, it would seem, never sleeps in Congress. This "wide-open socialistic subsidy formula" was condemned with much the same rhetoric used in regard to many federal housing programs over the last thirty years.

It is interesting to note that a Banking and Currency Committee pamphlet called a "committee print" was circulated by supporters of rent supplements in an attempt to refute these minority views. This print rebuttal clearly indicated the importance of the minority report; and the print itself became a focus of controversy in the ensuing House floor debate.

House Floor Debate

The minority report boded ill for the future of this omnibus housing bill. Floor debate on the bill was, if anything, more acrimonious and polarized. Most of the debate again focussed on Section 101. One of the most interesting issues raised in the House debate was the bold "new" character of the Rent Supplements Program (as the proponents described it) or its "revolutionary" and un-American character (as the opponents described it).[10] Just how new or revolutionary was the idea of federal rent subsidization? In the debates over public housing in the 1930s some business opponents of public housing both inside and outside

Congress saw it as a socialistic invasion of an area previously ruled by private enterprise. However, business and housing industry opponents of public housing did propose an alternative housing plan similar in several ways to the plan proposed by the Democratic administration. Although severely criticized by many Republicans and business conservatives during the 1965-69 debates, the idea of federal rent subsidization partially originated in their own ranks and was propagated by their own representatives—but in the 1930s. Although these early plans sometimes varied in detail, in mechanics, and in name, the general philosophy was to give the private market the chance to house low-income families by providing government-financed rent subsidies.

For example, one of the opponents of funding the Rent Supplements Program during the 1966 debates was the U.S. Chamber of Commerce. However, in the congressional hearings leading up to the U.S. Housing Act of 1937—the act which established a government authority to provide loans for conventional public housing projects—the chairman of the chamber's special committee on housing explained that the chamber felt it was a false assumption that the lowest income groups could be housed only in new housing such as the proposed government-subsidized public housing. Rather "the most effective way" to house low-income families was in the private housing market "through direct assistance to the rent of families."[11] When the Democratic administration suggested a proposal based on this same philosophy of direct rent assistance, the same Chamber of Commerce took an opposite stance. In an April 1966 statement before House subcommittee hearings on the 1967 appropriations bill the chamber recommended that the request for rent supplements be cut in its entirety, an indication of its opposition to federal assistance for low-income families.[12]

During the debates of the thirties several other business organizations, in addition to the chamber, supported rent subsidization plans. The U.S. Building and Loan League urged legislators to consider a policy of giving rent support directly to families who would then be able to rent private or public facilities.[13] In addition, a representative of the Construction League of the United States, a confederation of contractors, engineers, materials producers, and architects, strongly opposed the public housing program on the grounds that it competed with the development of low-income housing by the private sector. He admitted that the construction industry was aware of the need for rent support until the necessary private housing could be built; he too proposed that direct rent support of low-income families was the desirable alternative to a capital-subsidy public housing program, since it would stimulate private enterprise to develop the necessary housing. His concluding comments sound as though they might well have come from a current proponent of rent supplements legislation: "By this method of rental subsidy the Government pays the difference between an economic rent and what a family is able to pay, and, as the income of our lowest financial group increases and it is able to afford more rent, the burden on the Federal Government immediately decreases."[14]

Another prestigious private supporter of direct rent subsidies, at least by the early 1940s, was the National Association of Real Estate Boards (NAREB), a consistent opponent of public housing since its inception. A 1943 NAREB policy statement contended that assistance from public sources should be given directly to families who could not pay regular rents. As the NAREB viewed it, such assistance was adjustable to the needs of any given family and enabled the private market to handle the low-income housing problem. However, during the early House hearings on rent supplements the NAREB spokesman indicated that they did not favor the approach. But like numerous private organizations, they had come around to support of the supplements approach by 1968.[15]

Foreshadowed in the House Subcommittee hearings, other arguments for rent supplements crystallized in the House debates. There supporters began to emphasize certain key features of the legislation. Taking up Secretary Weaver's ploy, several congressmen emphasized that the rent supplements approach was strictly a private program, the purpose of the program being to enable private enterprise in the United States to meet the needs of the low- and low-middle-income families, to meet the long-standing goal of a safe, decent home for every American.[16] If implemented, this approach would increase the supply of standard housing available at reasonable rentals—through private, not public, resources. This emphasis among proponents on the private enterprise character of the Rent Supplements Program gradually led them to contrast, and even to criticize, the existing public housing program. Early in these debates proponents estimated that the annual subsidy for public housing runs $58 per month per unit, compared to a $40-per-month per unit cost under the Rent Supplements Program. Moreover, they argued that the public housing program had been unable to supply the necessary number of units.[17] Over 500,000 families were usually on the waiting list for public housing; yet only 24,000 public housing units were constructed in 1964. One congressman also noted that some of those now worried about the threat that the Rent Supplements Program poses for public housing have been antagonists of public housing in the past.[18] Oddly enough, such erstwhile opponents of public housing were initially joined by none other than the National Association of Housing and Redevelopment Officials in opposing rent supplements. Later, with the *fait accompli*, NAHRO came around to a position of cooperation with private housing officials to make the Rent Supplements Program work.[19]

In the floor debate proponents reemphasized the great housing need in this country, citing the large number of substandard units and the misery of many families in our urban slums. The approach would fight urban slums. But backers frequently found themselves on the defensive, defending among other things the HHFA administrator's integrity and the income limits of the present bill. They also found the antagonists of the new approach to be vigorous and virulent in their amplification of earlier arguments. Phrases such as "across the board economic integration," "grabbing power," "aimed at changing social patterns," "an attempt to make the Federal Government the landlord of the entire

American middle-class," "way of socialist state," "to force integration," "is the U.S. ready for collectivism?" clearly indicate the tone of much of the opposition. Proponents spent some time dealing with these emotional arguments, trying in effect to argue that it is not socialistic or collectivistic to involve private enterprise in housing families.

During the 1965 House floor debates opponents of rent supplements legislation further developed their arguments, most of which had been set forth in the minority report. In addition to the aforementioned emphasis on the revolutionary and un-American character of the legislation, opponents reiterated certain arguments made in that minority report, such as the exorbitant cost of the program over the next forty years, the high-income limits of the program, the apparent emphasis on economic integration, the destruction of individual initiative, and the "socialistic" philosophy behind rent supplements.[20] A variation on this latter argument emphasized the federal "subsidy" character of the Rent Supplements Program. It became clear in the debates that the term "subsidy" was anathema both to supporters and opponents alike. Administration officials carefully avoided the term, while opponents of the Rent Supplements Program used it as a weapon. However congressional supporters, as well as papers like *The New York Times*, from time to time in the 1965-69 debates pointed out that American agriculture, business, transportation, and housing had long depended on federal subsidies. A classic example was occasionally cited: middle-class FHA homeowners have been receiving housing subsidies for thirty years.

Several additional opposing arguments were given emphasis in the House debate. One was the assertion that the Rent Supplements Program was little more than a "power grab" on the part of the Housing administrator. Congressman Paul Fino (New York) said: "I think that is what the Housing Administrator had in mind all the time—far-reaching control that would extend into every nook and corner of American residential patterns."[21] A growing discussion of federalized residential patterns also characterized the debate in the House. Those opposed emphasized explicitly for the first time that the bill would foster *racial* integration as well as economic integration. Opponents argued that the government should not use the vehicle of housing to "force" racial integration. What had been an undertone of the talk about forced economic integration now surfaced; behind opposition to the bill, especially on the part of suburban congressmen, lay fear of racial integration.

Indeed, it was on this issue of rent supplements that the Democratic administration came closest to defeat in 1965 in the House. A Republican attempt to kill the Rent Supplements Provision of the bill was narrowly defeated in a 208-to-202 House vote. The omnibus housing bill itself was later passed by the whole house in a 245-169 roll call vote, but only after a compromise provision was adopted restricting rent supplements *only* to low-income families eligible for public housing. The very families excluded from the president's original proposal were now the only ones eligible. Who were the supporters and opponents in the moment of decision? *Congressional Quarterly* reported that 26 Republicans and 219 Democrats voted for the bill, while 109 Republicans, 52 southern Democrats, and 8 northern Democrats voted against the bill.[22] This vote came at the end of numerous days of vigorous debate over rent supplements; the low-income restriction apparently saved the bill from an untimely death.

The Senate

Meanwhile, after hearings in which arguments similar to those in the House were raised, the Senate Banking and Currency Committee approved the Senate version of the bill in the early part of the summer, but only after limiting the Rent Supplement Program to families who could qualify for public housing and increasing the percentage of a person's income going toward rent to 25 percent, as in the House version.[23] The Senate version also added national disaster victims to the list of eligible recipients. Backers in the Senate debate on the bill again extolled rent supplements as a basic tool to help relieve the problems of low-income housing, while opponents reiterated the arguments made earlier in the House, namely, its revolutionary and experimental character, its destruction of incentive, its aim to create socioeconomic integration. Support was expressed for limiting the program just to low-income families.[24] After an attempt to delete the rent supplements section was narrowly beaten back on a 40-47 roll call vote, the bill was passed by the Senate and sent along to conference. The conference bill was passed by the House and Senate in July 1965. With the president's signature the Rent Supplements Program soon became law.

A summary of the rent supplements section as finally passed by the House and Senate is appropriate at this point. Title 1 of the Housing and Urban Development Act of 1965 provided that the HHFA administrator could make rent supplement payments on behalf of qualified individuals who could not secure "standard" private accommodations at rents less than one quarter of their incomes. The supplements would enable recipients—whose incomes had to be equal to or less than those allowed for public housing tenants—to live in "standard" private housing. Only persons who were aged, handicapped, displaced by government action, victims of a natural disaster, or those occupying substandard housing could qualify for subsidies.[25] Payments made to the landlord of private housing on behalf of the tenant were tied to a tenant's income; if income goes up, the subsidy goes down. According to the final version of the restrictions, only housing built by nonprofit corporations, limited dividend corporations, or cooperatives and financed under the FHA market-interest rate mortgage insurance program for low- and moderate-income families would qualify. Five percent of the funds authorized for fiscal 1966 could go to housing financed by FHA insured below-market interest rate loans.[26] The act also stipulated that supplements could not be paid to families living in housing whose operating costs were greater than those of comparable housing in the same area. Although the Housing Act of 1965 had many different sections involving a heterogeneous collection of housing subsidies, direct and indirect, the debate had focussed most exclusively on the portion of Title 1 relating to rent supplements.[27] The final version was a patchwork quilt of compromises.

The Appropriations Debate: 1965

Congressmen opposed to the Rent Supplements Program were to have the last word in 1965. In the October debate on the general supplemental appropriations bill for fiscal 1966 providing funds for the Rent Supplements Program, congressional fears of integrated housing again surfaced. One Southern congressman expressed it thus: "It would appear . . . this program is going to be administered in a way to bring about or assist in integrating residential areas along social and economic lines."[28] Another congressman argued that the private owner is doomed to declining property values because of HHFA commitment to using rent supplements to foster equal opportunity in housing. He went on to express his fears about certain civil rights organizations: "Any nonprofit organization may develop a housing project under the rent subsidy program and that includes such nonprofit organizations as the NAACP, SNICK, church organizations, fraternal organizations, civic clubs. The civil rights groups have made no secret of the fact they intend to use the law to integrate American neighborhoods."[29]

Another major objection to funding the Rent Supplements Program had to do with asset limits. Congressman James Harvey (Michigan), who as it turned out was instrumental in deleting the rent supplements appropriation, was dissatisfied with the appropriation on the grounds that there were no adequate asset limits for potential recipients. Preliminary regulations issued by FHA were construed to mean that a family with assets of $25,000 would be eligible. For this reason Congressman Harvey requested that the appropriation be deleted from the bill.[30]

The general supplemental appropriations bill for fiscal 1966 was passed in the House, but the Rent Supplements Program appropriation was deleted. Several senators, as well as the administration, were critical of House action, suggesting that the asset debate was a red herring, for no poor family has the kind of assets, namely stocks and bonds, being discussed. But Republicans and dissident Democrats were to have their way; in October 1965 funds to begin operation of the program were denied. The Senate had agreed to funding, but Senate-House conferees killed the provision, arguing that this would give the administration time to develop "sound plans."[31]

The Second Supplemental Appropriations Bill

The third round of the battle over rent supplements began with President Lyndon Johnson's January 1966 message on housing and urban development; he specifically urged funding of the program. He later requested that Congress provide $30 million for the program in fiscal 1966.[32] In this round the proposal had more going for it. In the first place, HHFA had issued in December 1965 a new set of guidelines, clarifying previous ambiguities and answering previous Republican objections: the guidelines established specific income limits for admission to the program and limited total assets to $5000 for elderly tenants and $2,000 for all others.[33] In addition, the administrator of the new Department of Housing and Urban Development (HUD) reported that he had already received proposals for 70,000 units from all states, indicating a substantial national interest of private entrepreneurs in the program. Additional support for the program came from the civic and housing industry groups which were now supporting rent supplements; and in February, under the auspices of the Americans for Democratic Action, a letter from 100 urban experts to President Johnson in support of unrestricted funding of the program was released.[34]

House debate on the second supplemental appropriations bill for fiscal 1966 again raised the issue of asset limitations, with proponents of rent supplements pointing to the new HUD guidelines.[35] One important result of the new HUD guidelines was the switch of several previous opponents to support of the appropriation. Congressman James Harvey (Michigan), one of the key Republican figures in the 1965 fight to delete the appropriation, switched to support, citing the fact that HUD had set up the guidelines necessary to restrict the program to the most deserving families. Interestingly, in defending his switch he quoted from Senator Robert Taft's famous New York University Speech (1949):

Many have denounced public housing as a communistic or socialistic enterprise. Of course, to a certain extent it is true that it is socialistic in nature. But this question of socialism is a relative matter. We have long socialized our public education in the primary and secondary schools. We have socialized medical care to the extent that we provide medical care to the poor through public hospitals. But this does not mean we have socialized medical care as a whole, or the medical profession. The public housing program is in no sense a socialization of the building industry, or of the housing industry. It is intended to reach only those whose income is so low as to prevent their renting the minimum of decent housing.[36]

This quote of Mr. Conservative himself was alluded to by proponents of rent supplements several times in the debates to support their contention that subsidization of rents was *not* a "socialization" of the housing industry.

Several new arguments for the program were developed this time by supporters. A new emphasis was placed on the taxation advantages of rent supplements. Such housing, unlike public housing, would stay on the tax rolls—an argument with great appeal to business interests. Another quite important argument to be heard increasingly in the 1966-69 debates was that the riots, the upheavals in urban ghettos, were indicative of the dire distress of low-income citizens; one good reason to vote for rent supplements appropriations was the hopelessness of the low-income situation together with a need to give low-income families an alternative to violence. Opponents took issue with this, arguing that no legislation should be passed under threat of riots, as it were, "under the gun." In the debates, riots and Vietnam, domestic versus foreign troubles, butter versus guns, were juxtaposed several times, with opponents of rent supplements arguing that we could not afford additional domestic spending while Vietnam was consuming such a large percentage of our budget and proponents arguing that we cannot afford to temporize about the distress of the poor in our cities.[37]

In addition, those opposed to rent supplements also reiterated the argument about forced housing integration. Even the churches were attacked for encouraging integration by "scatteration."[38] However it was clear that those who feared that the plan would be used to foster integration had already won out in the House Appropriations Subcommittee, where a local control rider, restricting contracts to projects approved by local officials or part of a "workable community program" (also locally determined) had already been attached.[39] Such a proviso would effectively keep most rent supplements projects out of suburban areas and restrict them to higher-cost downtown property, probably in many cases prohibiting their construction at all. Representative William Ryan (New York) condemned such a legislative proviso and saw through the rationalizations for it, stating that the proviso was written into the legislation "to block the possible exodus of low-income families into communities outside the central core of our cities. Local officials in these lilywhite bedroom suburbs can be expected to exercise this veto power to prevent the have-nots from coming into the community with the haves."[40] Ryan tried to delete the local control proviso, but his amendment was defeated by a House voice vote.

In the final analysis, the local control rider saved the Rent Supplements Program. After the House Subcommittee on Independent Offices Appropriations had reduced the contract authority from the $30 million requested by the president to $12 million and had appended the local control proviso, a proviso originally developed for the first supplemental bill, the House voted to reject a recommittal motion designed to kill the low-income program.[41] It seems certain that the proviso secured certain key Southern votes for the bill. *Congressional Quarterly* quoted a key Southern congressman as saying that he had "no doubt that the amendment eased the feelings of a lot of congressmen—both North and South."[42] The administration played down this interpretation, emphasizing the switch of key Republicans such as Congressman James Harvey in insuring passage of the legislation.[43]

Thus for the first time in the history of the Rent Supplements Program it seemed that money might actually be available to subsidize the rent of low-income families, although some proponents believed that the local control proviso still might restrict the program severely. Any hopes that the Senate might eliminate this severe restriction were soon to be dashed. Although a small group of liberal senators issued a statement condemning the proviso, support for the local control proviso was quite strong in the Senate.[44] The urban crisis argument, the riots in New York and Los Angeles, were countered by opponents who emphasized the problem of inflation and spending for Vietnam. One somewhat new emphasis that developed in the Senate debate was on the long-range effect of improved housing conditions—reduced crime, lower rates of mental illness, improved health. One senator mentioned the sociological and psychological studies which had allegedly found that poor housing is correlated with high rates of illness.[45] Another weapon in the arsenal of the proponents during both the Senate and House debates on the second supplemental bill was the growing number of applications coming into HUD for rent supplements contracts, 561 applications for 100,000 units up to April 1966 from all fifty states and Puerto Rico.[46] However, even with the local control proviso, the attempt to delete the provision in the Senate was barely defeated by *one* vote.[47] A few weeks later both houses adopted the conference report on the bill, and the Rent Supplements Program finally had some limited contractual authority for fiscal 1966.[48]

The Appropriations Debate, 1967-69

In May 1966 House discussion of the fiscal 1967 appropriation for the Rent Supplements Program began. In June President Johnson continued his pressure for increased funding of the program by announcing rent supplements projects for twelve U.S. cities, including key areas of Los Angeles (Watts) and New York (East Harlem), the first projects actually funded under the program.[49] And available information increasingly pointed to a substantial national demand for the supplements program.

Although there was continued opposition in the House and Senate, the 1967 appropriation for new contractual authority was approved by both houses in the summer of 1966. Conservative opponents again pressed .or deletion of the $20 million authorization on several familiar grounds: inflation, recipient loss of incentive, the unproven character of the program, its probable use as part of an open housing thrust, and its tremendous expense over forty years.[50] Those opposed to the use of rent supplements also indicated their fear that the program would be extended to include middle-income families, perhaps a realistic fear given the initial form of the program and some ambiguous comments by administration officials. Proponents resurrected some of their earlier arguments: the freshness of the idea, the existence of federal subsidies to other segments of the U.S. population, the fact that we were spending billions for space adventure, the great need for low-income housing in our cities, and the general urban crisis. With House and Senate passage (August 1966) the program was to be operating in fiscal 1967 with a $2 million actual payment level and a $20 million contractual authority level. It should be noted that all of the earlier restrictions still applied, including the local control proviso.

The next major round in the rent supplements fight took place over the fiscal 1968 appropriations bill. The riots of the 1964-66 summers had provoked the president to take an even more aggressive position on the need for doing something about the oppressive ghetto conditions behind riots. In August 1966 at a news conference the president said, in regard to what the federal government could do,

The second thing [in addition to the Teacher Corps] they can do is the new idea of rent supplements, which we think offers us the greatest opportunity since FHA was endorsed in this country to provide decent housing for poor people. We have urged the Congress to adopt that principle, to embrace it.[51]

He made similar arguments in his late summer tour of the northeastern states.[52]

A second major intervening event was the 1966 congressional election, which saw the replacement of many liberal congressmen by conservatives. In its issue published after the November elections the *Congressional Quarterly* estimated that the 213 to 208 House lineup in favor of the Rent Supplements Program had shifted to 173 to 238, with opponents clearly in the majority. The lineup in the Senate was still close to 50 to 50.[53] It is not surprising then that the 1968 appropriation was in for trouble. A House committee reduced the president's $40 million request to $10 million in new contractual authority. And more words were again spilled over the program on the floor of Congress, a program which was rapidly becoming one of the most talked about housing programs in the history of the Congress. The issue in Congress was not just the level of funding but the basic philosophy behind the program, even in this the third fiscal year of the program.[54]

Advocates reiterated their arguments that the program was based on the sound idea of substituting private credit for public credit, that it was a new and imaginative approach to the problem of housing low-income families. As one congressman expressed it: "How are you going to avoid crime and violence when you use compromise as the basis for appropriating money with which to meet problems that badly need care?"[55] With this argument in mind some proponents called for a *much* higher level of funding for rent supplements. Backing up this point one supporter noted the growing demand up to the present; according to his figures contracts and reservations had been made (by April 1967) for 42,962 units.[56] Other proponents, reflecting the national climate, argued that something must be done for the black and other minority servicemen returning from Vietnam to the slums; the nation must redeem its promises of better housing, so that Vietnam veterans can return to live apart from urban decay. Several urban congressmen accused their antagonists of taking a very negative attitude toward the snowballing problems of an urbanized society. Opponents, on the other hand, repeated their contention that the "subsidy" program was radical, designed to alter the basic structure of American society; and to promote "social upheaval." The charge was made that HUD was consulting with Stokely Carmichael and other radical civil rights leaders on its housing programs. Several opponents also pointed to votes in various parts of the country on the issue of rent supplements; they argued that the basic idea had been rejected in referenda by the American people. Indeed, a few polls had revealed that no more than one-quarter of the residents of any congressional district approved of the basic idea.[57]

The net result of this debate was another defeat for the program. In May 1967 the House excised the administration's request for $40 million in new contractual authority. The new conservative congressmen elected in the November elections, together with long-term opponents, had shifted the discussion back to the fundamental philosophy of rent subsidization. Many Republicans again seemed to base their opposition on the philosophy level, not just on the appropriations level; substantial support for excision also came from Southern Democrats. However, in the summer of 1967 the more liberal Senate Appropriations Committee voted to approve the entire $40 million for new contractual authority, although even the supporters of the Rent Supplements Program recommended a new qualification. Interested agencies, including nonprofit ones, should make a substantial commitment to their projects; an appropriate commitment would be a 5 percent equity investment. Senators were disturbed that the program had not brought in as much private capital as had originally been intended.[58] Another interesting point brought up in the Senate debate was that of city size. One complaint about the program was that since 1966 it had benefited small cities more than it had large ones.[59]

Senate acceptance of the $40 million level necessitated that the bill be sent to a conference committee. The conference report allowed only $10 million for new rent supplements contractual authority.[60] In October 1967 Congress finally approved new funds for fiscal 1968, although the House vote margin was only fourteen votes.

The next round of the struggle began in January 1968, when President Lyndon Johnson in his State of the Union message proposed a ten-year program to provide 6 million units for low- and moderate-income families.[61] In a subsequent message to Congress the president asked that the Rent Supplements Program be extended to $65 million in new contractual authority for fiscal 1969. A House Committee cut that figure by 60 percent to $25 million; on the floor supporters beat back Republican attempts to reduce and delete the 1969 appropriation.

One way to secure a bird's-eye view of the turbulent 1966 to 1969 career of this particular program of rent support for low-income families is to tabulate presidential requests and congressional appropriations:

Year	Presidential Request	Congressional Allowance
Fiscal 1966 (First Supplemental Act)	$30,000,000	-0-
Fiscal 1966 (Second Supplemental Act)	$30,000,000	$12,000,000
Fiscal 1967	$35,000,000	$20,000,000
Fiscal 1968	$40,000,000	$10,000,000
Fiscal 1969	$65,000,000	$12,000,000

The president requested new contractual authority to the tune of $30 million in fiscal 1966, $35 million in fiscal 1967, $40 million in fiscal 1968, and $65 million in fiscal 1969. Presumably the administration intended the program to reach those maximum contract levels; this is clear from the president's statement in his 1965 message to Congress, in which he said that the program would finance 500,000 housing units over these four fiscal years. The final version of the 1965 Housing Act reduced the authorized limits so that the maximum aggregate level by fiscal 1969 was to be $150 million. In the 1965-69 appropriations struggles, as can be seen in the chart above, the actual contract levels allowed by Congress in the annual appropriation acts were much lower than the president's requests or the levels authorized by the 1965 Housing Act. Congress ignored President Johnson's first request for contract authority and then granted him 40 percent of his second request, 60 percent of his third request, 25 percent of his fourth request, and about 20 percent of his last request. Such results clearly indicate the verbal and actual power of the opposition to this approach to the low-income housing problem. Slowly and reluctantly, the Congress began to support the policy of drawing from public funds the difference between what poor families can afford to pay for housing and what it costs to provide them with sound dwellings in the private market. In the 1970s the Rent Supplements Program continues to be regularly funded, but at a relatively modest level.

Conclusion

This review of the arguments and controversy over the Rent Supplements Program well documents the contention that there are divergent perspectives among various lobbies and elites over how to solve America's low-income housing problem. This review also indicates that the debate over the Rent Supplements Program was a barometer of national social and political weather. The need for new legislation to deal with the growing urban crisis was reflected in the administration attempt to sell the Rent Supplements Program as a bold new approach to the problem; this in turn has provoked opponents to envisage the program as radical, socialistic, and un-American. Yet rent subsidization proposals go back for at least several decades.

Moreover, as the urban crisis grew, with the riots in the summers of the mid-1960s, the arguments for and against the legislation also escalated. As U.S. Vietnam involvement increased—and with it inflation—the arguments about too much spending, "guns and butter," were increasingly emphasized by opponents of the Rent Supplements Program. Perhaps most important, the turbulent history of President Johnson's program raised again and again the series of important questions which we suggested at the beginning of this chapter, ranging from the qualifications and character of subsidy recipients to questions of economic and racial integration. This was not the last time Washington, D.C. was to hear of these arguments, for many of them persist as United States housing policy moves into the decade of the seventies.

Given this contextual setting of the Boston experimental rent subsidy program, we can now proceed to delineate the character of that program and the evaluation study, with a view toward many of the critical housing questions raised in the congressional controversy over rent supplements.

4

The Boston Experiment and Its Evaluation

The Boston Program

The Boston rent subsidy program dealt with a common situation in what may very well become a typical way. Of course the designers of the program did not realize how representative it would become when they were making their plans in 1963; the deliberate linking of rent supplements, newly built middle-income housing, and relocation of families displaced by renewal in the 1965 Housing Act hardly seemed likely then. But the Boston program's main features were prophetic:

1. The provision of housing for families displaced by public action, essentially by urban renewal.
2. Large families, with incomes low enough to admit them to public housing, and almost all black.
3. The use of direct rent subsidies.
4. The dwellings to be a minority of the units in newly constructed middle-income housing built by limited-profit corporations.
5. Housing built on a renewal site, and consequently in or near the ghetto.

This combination of circumstances promises to be a typical situation for the use of rent subsidies in American cities over the next few years. The Boston Housing Authority put together a prototype of a national program.

Let us look at those main features a little more closely. The BHA's commitment to the federal government was actually to give priority to families displaced by renewal rather than to restrict the rent subsidies to them. With only forty rent subsidies to offer, and thousands of families being displaced, the distinction did not matter much. Again, nothing in the formal language of the program singled out blacks. If there had been such a provision, many people would have considered it discriminatory. But the disproportionate poverty of Boston's blacks, the locations of the new housing developments involved, and the geography of renewal in Boston combined to make it virtually certain that most of the clientele would be blacks.

The provisions that the families be large and have low incomes, on the other end, figured explicitly in the plan. "Large" meant families requiring three or more bedrooms (by public housing standards, which take the composition of the household into account but rarely assign a three-bedroom unit to a family of

67

fewer than five persons). "Low income" meant one thing for admission to the program and another thing for remaining in it. This table summarizes the maximum income limits in effect as the program began:

	Maximum Income Limits For Admission to the Program		Maximum Income Limits for Retention
Number of Persons	Families Displaced by Renewal	Others	All Families
4	$4,750	$3,800	$5,225
5-6	5,125	4,100	5,638
7 or more	5,500	4,400	6,050

Roughly speaking, then, the program excluded families earning more than $1,200 per person per year; the larger the family, the lower the per-person limit. This meant that it applied to families which would ordinarily have no chance of renting new housing and little chance of renting standard housing in the Boston market.

Tying the rent support to apartments in new middle-income developments also added something to the Boston experiment. Three developments were involved. We shall describe them later on. For the moment, the important things to know about them are that they were all on the Washington Park renewal site (and were, in fact, the first new housing to go up after clearance of the site), that they were sponsored by organizations—churches and a union—strongly committed to that section of the city, and that "middle-income" families were to occupy nine-tenths of the apartments. The ceilings on income for the larger families were:

4 persons	$ 7,700.00
5-6 persons	8,850.00
7 or more	10,000.00

Note: The limits ran about $500 lower in one of the developments.

The rents of $85 to $147 per month made it almost impossible for a family with less than $5,000 per year to get in. While there could be a little overlap in aggregate income between the families in the subsidy program and their neighbors, they were destined on the average to be significantly poorer than the rest.

The location of the three new developments on the renewal site—two of them in its heart, the other at its edge—also placed them in the ghetto. Since it was attractive housing, conveniently located for people working in central Boston and moderately priced, there was some chance that it would attract white newcomers to the city or whites from elsewhere in the metropolitan area. Still, the location in the ghetto, the deliberately nondiscriminatory rental policies, the pent-up. demand for good housing among black families, and the developers' obligation to give preference to families displaced by urban renewal all added up to a predominantly black group of tenants. In fact, 400 of the first 464 families to move into the three developments were black, and at least 15 more were interracial; turnover during the first two years produced an even higher proportion of blacks.

Finally, the location of the new housing meant that the area was already familiar to most of the residents long before they moved in. They were not like new suburbanites. Of course, the spanking-new buildings were unlike anything else in the Washington Park area, and the wreckers had erased many of the old familiar sights. But most of the new residents—middle-income and low-income alike—had lived nearby and knew the lay of the land. In these respects, they had less to learn than the average arrival in a newly built subdivision.

The greatest novelties the low-income families faced were new housing and an exceptional social situation. We can sum up the unusual effects of the subsidy program by saying that it provided new housing in the ghetto to large, poor, black families and gave them neighbors (including a small minority of middle-income whites) who were substantially better off than they were. Not surprisingly, this combination of events has *rarely* occurred before in the United States.

Many people had a part in the operation of the program. The Boston Housing Authority provided the original formal proposal, sought the federal funds, and set up an important part of the administrative apparatus; but the working out of the plan, the selection of the families, and the operation of the program took the cooperation of the developers of the 221 (d) (3) housing, the Boston Redevelopment Authority, and several other organizations.

To be more exact, the planning of the program required a whole series of agreements between the BHA and the private developers; since they thought of the subsidy program as a way of meeting their relocation needs, officials of the Boston Redevelopment Authority (BRA) were also involved. As it turned out, two main points took a great deal of negotiating: the selection of the families and the provision of information for this evaluation. In the first case, the developers sought guarantees that they would not have "problem" families on their hands to jeopardize the success of their projects, the BHA sought guarantees that the families receiving subsidies would receive equal treatment and that they would be families normally eligible for public housing, while the BRA sought a part in the selection of the families. The outcome, cumbersomely but no doubt predictably, was that all three tried to screen the applicants separately.

In principle, providing information for our systematic evaluation presented no problem to the BHA, worried the developers somewhat, and bothered the BRA officials a great deal. The responsible BRA officials found our request for access to relocation records hard to take; we gathered that the widespread past criticism of the BRA's relocation efforts made them reluctant to open the records to outsiders. In fact, we never did get permission to study relocation records, although we were eventually able to gain information about families likely to join the subsidy program from BRA relocation workers.[a] With this exception, however, the problems of getting access to information in the files of the organizations involved in the program eventually came to look quite small compared to the practical difficulties of diverting to research needs the information-gathering routines that the BHA, the BRA, and the developers had set up for administrative purposes.

Since there were two developers, three sponsors of developments, and numerous organizations somehow involved, this planning and negotiation continued even after the first families in the program entered their new housing in the summer of 1964. The discussions went on most of the year.

Selection of the Families

By that time, the second main phase of the program's operation, the selection of the families, was well underway. While there were many variations, a common sequence was for the BRA workers at the Washington Park site to propose families for whose relocation they were responsible, for the BHA tenant selection officers to examine the families' dossiers to determine their legal eligibility, then find out whether the family was interested, next forward family and information to the developer for screening, then complete the tedious verifications of eligibility through checks on income, previous residence, and so on, and finally sign an agreement with the developer and arrange for the moving of the family. Another common sequence was for the BHA's own tenant selection office to spot an applicant for public housing who had been displaced by urban renewal, and then to move on as before. In a few other cases, the developer himself received an application from a prospective tenant whose income was low enough to make him eligible for a rent subsidy and therefore contacted the BHA.

This description deals with the selection process from a bureaucratic viewpoint. From the point of view of the family, it was more like this: at some point in a search for housing they had already begun, someone (most likely a BRA relocation worker, a BHA tenant selection officer, or the person taking applications for one of the developers) suggested the program, and they expressed interest. They were soon subjected to a series of interviews in various offices, then experienced several months of uncertainty while they received fragmentary (or no) information about their own eligibility, about available apartments, about moving dates and many other crucial items, and finally went through a great rush as they got final word and prepared to move.

---

[a]For this reason, we had to abandon our hope of making detailed comparisons between the families in our study and all families displaced by the Washington Park renewal program.

From either perspective, there was clearly little opportunity for families deliberately to seek out the subsidy program, but some opportunity for the agencies involved to block a given family from entering it. Although the interests and criteria of the three veto-holders differed, the net effect was to shunt aside extremely "risky" or "undesirable" families.

This process of selection was going on actively from the summer of 1964, when the first prospects for subsidized apartments in the development called Marksdale Gardens signed up, to the summer of 1965, when the last tenant to receive a rent subsidy while living in the large development called Academy Homes was selected. The third phase—the operation of the rent subsidies themselves—began shortly after. The first families in the program moved into Marksdale Gardens in August 1964. The last of the forty-family contingent was not settled in new housing until the fall of 1965.

This third, administrative, phase of the program chiefly involved the BHA and the private managers of the new housing. But there were others. Action for Boston Community Development, an organization set up to work closely with the BRA on the "human problems of urban renewal," set up a special office with caseworkers and volunteers assigned to help the families in the new developments. They emphasized housekeeping problems, and referred other difficulties to a wide range of specialized agencies. The BRA's Washington Park Multi-Service Center likewise had caseworkers in the new developments. Members of both these agencies, for example, entered the operation of the subsidy program as informants and mediators in 1966, when the manager of one of the developments decided to evict three of the families in the program for "bad housekeeping" and a variety of other offenses. But for most of the families the operation of this phase of the subsidy program was invisible. It consisted simply of the BHA sending a monthly check to the property manager, covering the difference between the stated rent of the apartment the family occupied and the amount they themselves paid the manager, which was, of course, the amount they would have paid in public housing.

Our Observation Study

Our last major contact with the families came in the summer of 1966, so for our purposes the third phase ended then. We might summarize the schedule as follows:

Phase I	Planning and negotiation	all of 1964
Phase II	Selection of tenants	June 1964 to June 1965
Phase III	Administration of program	August 1964 to June 1966

Since we did not begin work until June 1964, we missed an important part of the planning and negotiation. Our evaluation covers the two years from then until June 1966.

As is all too often the case, the comprehensive evaluation plan we had in mind at the start turned out to be impossible to achieve. It centered on two features: the comparison of matched samples and the gathering of information from each family through a series of interviews bracketing their move. The matched-sample design called for the comparison of the forty families in the rent subsidy program with forty similar families in each of the following categories:

Middle Income: other families moving into the same middle-income developments at the same time, similar in age and size, but not receiving rent subsidies.

Public Housing: other poor families moving into public housing at the same time.

Private Market: other poor families finding housing in the private market at the same time.

From each of these categories we planned to select one family matched with each of the forty in the subsidy program. They were to be similar in terms of color, size, composition, time of move into new housing, area of the city moved from, and (except for the middle-income group) income.

The interview plan divided the families into three groups, depending on when they were expected to move:

Group A consisted of 7 families expected to move into Marksdale Gardens in the late spring of 1964, plus 21 other families (in three groups of seven each) matched with them; we planned to interview them about six weeks after the move and again six months later.[b]

Group B consisted of 15 families entering Marksdale Gardens and Charlame Park in fall and winter 1964, plus 45 families matched with them; we planned to interview them about six weeks before moving, about six weeks after moving, and again six months later.

Group C consisted of 18 families scheduled to move into Academy Homes in the spring of 1965, plus 54 families matched with them; we planned to interview them about six weeks before moving and about six weeks after moving.

This made a projected total of 380 interviews for 160 families.

In addition to this central interviewing program, we planned to talk to many workers in organizations coming into contact with the program in one way or

---

[b]When the BHA invited us to undertake the evaluation, the organization of the program and the construction of the new housing were already well advanced. It seemed likely that families would be moving in within a few weeks, too soon for us to organize interviews. The unanticipated delays in construction and administration so familiar to people in housing programs, however, actually gave us time to see the first group of families before they moved.

another, to interview a number of local leaders in the Roxbury ghetto area, to keep in touch informally with some families in the new developments to watch the BHA's administration of the program from day to day, to extract information about the families in our survey from such records as public housing application files, and to assemble background data concerning the housing situation of Boston's large, low-income black families from other agencies and from published sources.

In principle, the plan for multiple interviews with matched samples is very attractive. The easier and more common housing research procedure of interviewing representative samples of residents in each of several different kinds of housing *after* they have moved in leaves great doubt as to how much of the difference between one housing group and another is due to the selection of types of people who were already distinct before they moved in, and how much of what people say in retrospect about the old neighborhood really reflects their experience in the new one. The multiple-interview-matched-sample design reduces those doubts. But it rests, as we learned to our chagrin, on several risky assumptions:

1. That the investigator is able, well in advance, to identify and describe the people in the group with which the others are to be matched.
2. That somewhere in each population from which the matching groups are to come there will be at least one family similar to each family in the group with which the others are to be matched.
3. That the investigator is able to identify and describe *those* people well in advance.
4. That he knows when all the families will move.

Every one of these assumptions turned out to be partly wrong.

Because of the complicated selection process we have already described, it often happened that no one knew whether a given family would be in the rent subsidy program until two or three short weeks before they moved into their new housing. This often occurred at a moment when there was no middle-income family with similar characteristics left to move into the same development. Furthermore, the waiting time for large apartments in public housing was so great that while there were plenty of similar families on the waiting list, very often none of them reached the head of the list within a month or so of the rent subsidy program.

The BRA's refusal to let us work directly with relocation records and the highly decentralized operation of its Washington Park relocation office both made it very hard to identify and describe poor families displaced by urban renewal who were about to move into the private market. Finally, in the BHA's tenant selection office and elsewhere, we discovered that the best-informed officials could rarely predict moving dates with a margin of error of less than a month.

This last difficulty created a class of respondents we had not planned for and did not really want: the nonmovers. They were the families who were identified as "about to move" at some point in the study, who were chosen to match one of the families in the subsidy program, but who were still in their old dwellings when the study ended. There were thirty-four of them, most of them originally identified by the BHA's tenant selection office as about to move into public housing.[c] The second largest group were looking for housing in the private market with BRA help. These immobile families provided a new kind of control. Their experiences offered some lessons about the consequences of urban renewal and relocation—or rather nonrelocation—we would not otherwise have had. Nevertheless, their loss seriously depleted our "public housing" and "private mover" categories. So the painfully short supply of large units in public housing and of adequate housing in the private market hurt our respondents and our study at the same time.

One more assumption which caused trouble was that the developers and the BHA would keep to the original schedule. We can point up the optimism of that assumption by laying out the expected and actual moving dates of the three main groups:

Group	Expected to Move In	Actually Moved In
A	Late Spring 1964	August 1964
B	Fall and Winter 1964	January-June 1965
C	Spring 1965	July-October 1965

With unlimited research time and funds, this average delay of about four months would not have been serious. We had neither the funds nor the personnel to keep our research organization going past midsummer 1966, so the delay meant curtailing some of the work originally planned. The most important loss was the dropping of the third interview for about forty of the roughly ninety families with whom we had planned to do the full set of three. More precisely, we completed the relatively brief interview intended for six weeks after the move with the fifty-two families in the entire sample who had moved by the end of March 1965, and later interviewed all but two of them again at greater length. The families who moved later were only interviewed twice, and at length: before and after the move.

We offer these details as explanations for some of our departures from the original design and as warnings to other research evaluators who face the same situation.[1] Although at times we felt mightily frustrated by the obstacles to the

---

[c]The tenant selection office sent us capsule descriptions of each family assigned to a project as the assignments were made and the records sent to the project office. At that time they made the assignments to projects on the basis of probable, not actual, vacancies, in order to make it easier for managers to fill vacancies quickly. Their system also gave more discretion to the managers, and more uncertainty to the tenant selection officers.

needs of research posed by the people and the procedures of the government agencies we were working with, it was not just their inefficiency but also our optimistic assumptions that brought us into difficulty.

Our largest error was no doubt to assume that the information was there, accessible, in usable form. In large operating agencies like the BHA and the BRA, the kind of continuous and systematic information which lends itself to an estimate of the effects of a given program almost never accumulates in central files, the personnel have little interest or skill in collecting or communicating that sort of information, and long experience with the use of such information as a political weapon breeds widespread resistance to the communication of operating information. Asking for predictions of events over which the agency has only partial control simply adds to the difficulties. The investigator who wants to win out over these difficulties has three main choices: collect his own information independently, figure out a way to use information already being generated within the organization without insisting on new procedures, or take part himself in the planning and the operation of the organization (or perhaps of the particular program under scrutiny).

Our responses combined all three of these tactics with some changes in the design of the evaluation. Although they consumed a large part of our energy for two years, the various stratagems we finally used to assemble advance information about potential respondents are too various, too local in application, and too boring to impose on our readers. The only one that needs mentioning is our practice of interviewing "on speculation." As one pool or another of potential matching families (for example, middle-income families moving into one of the new developments) began to dry up before we knew who the corresponding families in the rent subsidy program would be, we interviewed as many as possible of the families in that pool who were likely to be similar to the subsidy families finally chosen. This meant, of course, wasting a good many interviews; the alternative was to lose all chance of matching and comparison.

Our Analysis

So much for what we could not do. What we did was to hold on to the basic plan, accept a looser form of matching than we had hoped for, cut down on some of the families who were meant to have three regular interviews and conduct only two with them, add premove interviews with the first group of respondents, add a special set of sixty-one follow-up interviews with families in the subsidy program and their middle-income neighbors, and conduct the supplementary gathering of data more or less as planned. (Note that interviews were conducted with wives.)

A compact tabulation will sum up the most important interviews:

Category	Long Interviews Shortly Before Moving	Long Interviews Some Time Later	Short Follow-Ups May and June 1966
Families in the rent subsidy program	40	40	29
Families moving into public housing	33	31	0
Families moving in the private market	17	17	0
Families waiting to move	34	24	0
Middle-income families moving into 221 (d) (3)	58	50	32
Totals	182	162	61

Out of the 182 households interviewed at least once before the June 1966 follow-ups, there are only five sets of families satisfactorily matched across all four basic categories—instead of the forty originally planned. Because of the small number of families who actually found housing in the private market, even the pairing of categories instead of taking them four at a time provides only seventeen matches in one important group of comparisons.

Fortunately, the general procedure for selecting the sample made the critical aggregate characteristics of the major categories of respondents quite similar to each other and thus provided a crude match. We have, that is, approximately the same samples we would have assembled if our plan had simply been to draw from each of the pools (people currently moving into public housing, people currently moving in the private market, people entering the 221 (d) (3) projects) all the large families displaced by urban renewal. In most of our later comparisons, we have fallen back on that crude matching of the major categories in order to be able to examine more cases than the family-by-family matching would permit. Furthermore, we have restricted many of the comparisons to the set of 120 black families for whom we have satisfactory before—and—after interviews, because we have greater confidence in their comparability than in the case of the white and interracial families. We have tried, however, to be sure that any results to which we attach particular importance show up in both the crude comparisons and the fine ones.

By taking this tack, we have reluctantly sacrificed statistical purity, but we have gained one small bonus: the ability to compare the original four sets of movers with the important group of respondents we did not expect to have, those who did not move at all. In some respects, as we shall show later on, they were the greatest victims of clearance and relocation.

We have already discussed the objectives of our evaluation in general terms. They were to assess the effectiveness of the Boston rent subsidy program with particular emphasis on what the families in the program experienced as compared with similar families taking the other main housing alternatives open to them; to judge in more general terms the utility of rent subsidies as part of public policy for housing in Boston and elsewhere; to learn how low-income and middle-income families respond to living as neighbors in similar housing; to gain a clearer understanding of just what barriers and alternatives poor black families in big cities face in their search for housing; to examine the impact of relocation (and of relocation into substantially different sorts of neighborhoods) on the social lives of poor families; and to add to available systematic knowledge of the character of social life in working-class black neighborhoods.

With respect to housing, public policy, and the operation of the Boston demonstration program, the BHA and the federal government had a more specific but no less ambitious set of questions in mind. They asked us to gather evidence on the following matters:

1. The development of methods and procedures and administrative forms and records;
2. The costs per unit of demonstration housing as compared to regular public housing costs;
3. The effectiveness with which the inventory of housing can be expanded by the proposed methods;
4. The degree of acceptance, particularly by neighbors paying full economic rents in the housing developments, of low-income families assisted by rent subsidy in non-public housing environments;
5. The effects of different housing accommodations on the social adjustments of low-income families;
6. The quality of household maintenance under the varying housing methods;
7. Rent-paying patterns and relationship to types of housing; and
8. Other differences in pertinent aspects of living a) in private housing with rental assistance, b) in public housing, and c) in private housing without rent supplementation, that will reflect on the relative merits of the three housing methods.[2]

We have some evidence on all these points, and more. The remaining chapters present and assess the evidence. Chapter 5 describes the people who entered the rent subsidy program and the new housing developments they moved into, and it offers some preliminary comparisons between them and the other groups of people we followed. Chapters 6 and 7 study the impact of the move and of the new location on the different groups of movers, as well as the relations between middle-income and low-income neighbors. Chapter 8 broadens the inquiry to the administration of the subsidy program, its impact on the public and on the housing market, its costs and benefits as public policy. Chapter 9, finally, summarizes the findings and presents our conclusions and recommendations systematically.

5

The Areas and Their People

Segregation

Our experience in conducting this evaluation research sums up an important feature of most attempts to examine and ameliorate ghetto life: the way they work from the outside in. Even though many of the people who worked on our study were blacks, only a few of üs lived in or near the ghetto, or even had very great familiarity with that section of Boston. When we went to talk with officials of agencies operating programs of intervention in the ghetto, we usually went to offices in parts of the city where we saw very few black faces. When we took the bus to Roxbury from Cambridge or some other suburban location, we passed through barriers of solid apartments and lofty office buildings before the steady change in passengers—white faces getting off, black faces getting on—and more rapid change of the physical surroundings—grimy stores, lofts, boarded-up apartments, empty lots—told us we were entering a new sort of community. Later we saw more of the variety, and more of the beauty, of the ghetto. But for us it was only part of a much larger world. For most of the families into whose lives we were inquiring, on the other hand, central Boston and its small black offshoot contained most of the social world.

At the time when we first contacted them in 1964 and 1965, almost all the families who gave us information lived in Roxbury, Dorchester, or the South End. They lived in or on the fringe of Boston's ghetto. More exactly, the numbers were as follows:

	Fourteen Ghetto Tracts	Other South End	Other Roxbury	Other Dorchester	Other Boston	Total
Black	115	1	21	16	4	157
White	19	0	3	0	3	25
Total	134	1	24	16	7	182

About three-fourths of the black families, and a roughly similar proportion of the white and mixed families, were living in the fourteen census tracts which already had black majorities in 1960. The proportions varied in an interesting way among the groups which later ended up in different types of housing. Taking only the 120 black families and 9 white or mixed families on which most of our discussion will focus, the proportions starting out in the fourteen central ghetto tracts were these:

79

Group	Description	Total Number	Percentage in Central Ghetto Tracts
Private	Black families who moved into private housing	16	81%
Public	Black families who moved into public housing	24	62
Subsidy	Black families who moved into 221 (d) (3) housing and received rent subsidies	35	92
Middle income	Black families who moved into 221 (d) (3) housing and paid full rent	29	48
Nonmovers	Black families who had not moved from their original residence at the time of the final interview	16	87
Whites	All white and mixed families	9	67
Total		129	70%

The middle-income families most frequently lived outside the heart of the ghetto. This does not really mean they lived in stably integrated areas; fourteen of the fifteen middle-income families living just outside the central ghetto tracts were in fast-changing areas of Dorchester, Roxbury, and the South End. Nevertheless, their relatively greater contact with integrated living set them off from their future low-income neighbors, of whom nine-tenths lived in the central ghetto and the other tenth in immediately adjacent areas.

Table 5-1 tells us that this contrast between where the two groups lived was part of a larger difference in their experience with integration. The table presents both statements of preference and reports on contacts with whites. The members of all black groups overwhelmingly rejected segregated neighborhoods, but a few of the subsidy group expressed a preference for the ghetto. There was little difference among the groups in the proportions with children in predominantly white schools. Few families in any group received sociable visits from whites; to our surprise, the subsidy wives reported such visits a bit more frequently than the other groups did. When given the choice of identifying themselves with a Roxbury white or a Washington, D.C., black, the middle-income women most frequently chose the local white, the nonmovers the distant black, and the other groups clustered in between.

The largest differences appeared in terms of the respondent's own childhood school experience and current work experience. A majority of the middle-income respondents said they had gone to predominantly white elementary schools, while only a fifth of the subsidy respondents had done so. Likewise, a majority of the middle-income respondents (or their husbands, where the husbands were the breadwinners) worked in predominantly white organizations, while less than a third of the subsidy breadwinners did so.[a]

We might sum up the situation before the move in this way: on the whole, middle-income families had the greatest contact with whites; subsidy families generally had the least contact with whites; but the differences were neither large nor consistent.

For the sample as a whole, the net effect of the moves we were observing was to move people out of the ghetto core into its periphery. Because it is so hard to estimate the proportions of blacks in the areas adjacent to the old ghetto in 1964 or 1965, it is difficult to say whether this outward movement actually produced some desegregation. The black respondents' own reports after the move suggest some increase in contacts with whites. The percentages of each of the black groups in the fourteen census tracts of the ghetto core before and after the move were as follows:

	Private (N=16)	Public (N=24)	Middle Income (N=29)	Subsidy (N=35)	Nonmover (N=16)	Total (N=120)
Before	81	62	48	92	87	73
After	50	12	58	49	87	49

Because two of the three 221 (d) (3) developments went up in the midst of the old ghetto's urban renewal area, the middle-income families experienced a net movement into the old ghetto. The nonmovers, of course, stayed in place. The other three groups moved outward. Essentially because (despite the relative segregation of the projects themselves) virtually none of Boston's public housing is in the ghetto core, those who moved into public housing most regularly moved away. Data not presented here show that the families moving into public housing moved a greater average distance than the rest.

But where did most people go? To the areas into which the ghetto was already expanding. For all 120 black families, here are the numbers in each of the major dwelling areas before and after the move:

---

[a]The largest part of this difference is due to the fact that more of the subsidy breadwinners were unemployed, yet the difference still shows up among those who were at work. In either case, the effect was for the middle-income people to have more contacts with whites. The results are, of course, quite different for the small number of whites in the sample; they lived in a mainly white world even though many of their children went to mainly Negro schools.

Table 5-1
Contact with Whites (and Blacks) before Moving

	Private Movers N = 16	Public Movers N = 24	Subsidy N = 35	Middle Income N = 29	Nonmovers N = 16	Whites N = 9
"Would you prefer to live in a neighborhood where almost everyone is a black, almost everyone is white, or in a mixed neighborhood?" Percentage replying "mixed" or "it makes no difference."	100%	96%	89%	100%	100%	67%
"About how many of the students in the elementary school which you attended were whites?[a] Would you say a few, more than a few but less than half, or more than half?" Percentage replying "more than half."	38	42	20	62	44	0
"About how many of the students which your oldest child now goes to school with are white? . . ."[a] Percentage replying "more than half."	25	21	26	24	31	44
"About how many of the people you (your husband) work with are white? . . ."[a] Percentage replying "more than half."	56	42	29	69	44	12

"How often do white[a] people visit in your home socially?" Percentage replying "often," "very often," "once or twice a month," "once or twice a week."	12	17	23	17	19	22
"Which of these two people do you think you have more in common to talk about with? A white person who lives in Roxbury, or a black person who lives in, say, Washington, D.C.?" Percentage replying "Black in Washington."	56	58	60	48	75	11

[a]"Black" for white respondents.

	Fourteen Ghetto Tracts	Other Roxbury	Other Dorchester	Other Boston	Total
Before	88	15	12	5	120
After	59	43	14	4	120

These data permit us to state more precisely the net geographic effect of the moves made by our black families: it was to displace them from the central ghetto to adjacent sections of Roxbury. An important part of that shift came from the moving of thirty families into one of the 221 (d) (3) developments, Academy Homes, which is actually located on the edge of the ghetto, and is itself around nine-tenths black. And the rest came essentially from the families moving to public housing which, as we have seen, was also quite segregated. In short, the moves made by our families followed the same pattern as those of all the families displaced by the Washington Park renewal program. Instead of a breakup of the ghetto, they amounted to its displacement into other housing areas.

Yet our respondents tended to report that the new environment was somewhat less segregated than the old. We asked three of the questions about experience with whites in identical form before and after the move. The responses from the black respondents came out like this:

		Private (N=16)	Public (N=24)	Middle Income (N=29)	Subsidy (N=35)	Nonmover (N=16)	Total (N=120)
Percentage saying "more than half" the students that the oldest child now goes to school with are white	Before	25	21	24	26	31	25
	After	25	42	52	31	38	38
Percentage saying "more than half" the people at workplace are white[a]	Before	56	42	69	29	44	47
	After	50	38	59	31	50	44
Percentage saying whites visit in home "often," "very often," "once or twice a month," "once or twice a week"	Before	12	17	17	23	19	18
	After	38	21	42	37	25	33

[a]Figures shown here are for all black families, including those with no employed person, on the grounds that this better represents the extent to which families have contacts with whites through the workplace. The proportions calculated for those at work only are, of course, higher: 76 percent before, 72 percent after, but the pattern is virtually the same.

Relatively few of the breadwinners changed jobs between the two interviews, and the reports on workplaces stayed about the same. Most families, however, changed schools, and all but the nonmovers changed neighbors. In both respects, the reports of contact with whites generally went up. The most notable case was that of the middle-income families, who reported much whiter schools and more social contact with whites. We should not treat these figures as strict representations of the facts, however: the children of the subsidy families were generally going to the same schools as those of the middle-income families, yet their mothers reported lower proportions of whites in the schools; and even the nonmovers' reports of white contacts drifted up a bit from the first interview to the second. Later on we shall examine what sorts of changes in social life the move brought to the various categories of families. For the moment, we can say for the sample as a whole that the move out of slum housing also meant a small move away from the heart of the ghetto and away from intensely segregated social life. In terms of sheer location, the families moving to public housing made the greatest break with the ghetto, if not with segregation. But in more general terms, the total extent of desegregation of any of the groups was equally small.

The Groups under Study

In terms of objective characteristics like age and income, the different housing groups resembled each other. We had, of course, deliberately matched all but the middle-income families on size, income, and household composition. For that reason our findings give us no warrant to conclude that people who move into public housing generally resemble people who move in the private market. Since, however, our fine matching procedures broke down for reasons we have already discussed, and since later comparisons of the experiences of families who moved into different kinds of housing will depend to some extent on the assumption that the families were similar before they moved, it is important to check the objective characteristics of those families.

The average woman we interviewed was a little over thirty years of age, a native of the South who had not completed high school, the mother of four or five children. About half the time there was no adult male in the household, and the woman herself headed the household. There were some variations from category to category which could result from selective recruitment of families into one housing situation or another. The middle-income families, as expected, had slightly more education than the rest. In other respects—even in terms of income—they resembled the rest of the sample more closely than one would imagine. The few white households in the sample were younger, smaller, and better educated than the average; again the differences were small.

Public housing drew an exceptional proportion of impoverished, female-headed households, while private housing drew more than its share of native Bostonians. The subsidy families were especially likely to be Southern migrants with large families. But the group which stood out most from the rest was the nonmovers: families scheduled to enter public housing or to find private housing with the aid of the Boston Redevelopment Authority who were still in their original dwellings at the end of our study. There the profile of the typical respondent would go something like this: a thirty-seven-year-old Southern-born mother of five children who went through one year of high school, deserted by her husband and living on an income of $4,000 per year, mostly from public assistance of one variety or another. Except for the middle-income group, none of our families was in *remotely* comfortable circumstances. But the public housing families and, especially, the nonmovers seemed worse off than the rest (see Table 5-2).

Nevertheless, the families in our four basic housing categories had a lot in common. Although they may have distinguished themselves in subtler ways, the families selected for the experimental rent subsidy program had no obvious characteristics making them likely prospects for new housing. That matters, because after moving out of their old places they reported rather different experiences from the other low-income groups.

A few thumbnail sketches will make the range of people in the rent subsidy program clear:

Table 5-2
General Characteristics of Major Housing Groups

	Private	Public	Subsidy	Middle Income	Nonmover	White	Total
Number	16	24	35	29	16	9	129
Percentage of respondents born in Boston area	38	25	17	31	19	33	
Percentage of households headed by females	48	62	40	38	56	11	
Median number of persons per household	6.5	5.0	7.0	6.0	6.5	5.0	
Median school years completed by household head	11.0	11.0	10.0	12.0	9.5	12.0	
Median year of birth of respondents	1933	1933	1932	1931	1927	1936	
Median family income in previous year	$4250	$3000	$4000	$5500	$4000	$3800	

1. The family of Mr. and Mrs. A. moved into their six-room home in Academy Homes in August 1965. Both in their early thirties, James and his wife are the black parents of six children, aged 2 to 15. A high-school freshman dropout, Mr. A. has been employed by the U.S. Navy for 15 years as a launderer and storekeeper in ship's service. He makes $450 per month. Mrs. A. is now a housewife, but hopes to apply for a job as a stitcher to add to her husband's income.

2. The family of Mr. and Mrs. B. moved into Academy Homes in August 1965. Blacks originally from Georgia, the B's came to Boston in 1953. They are the parents of three girls and three boys, ages 5 to 15. Mr. B., in his early forties, completed the ninth grade. He is presently employed by the Naval shipyard as a steel charger. Mrs. B., in her late thirties, left high school in her junior year. She is a shoe stitcher, but seeks a higher position as a postal clerk. Already she has taken the civil-service examination. The monthly family income is $400.

3. Mrs. C., a black divorcee, came to Boston in 1955 from Mississippi. Dissatisfied with past landlords and high rents, she was eager to move into Academy Homes with her eight children. Since her entry in October 1965, a younger sister has come from the South to live with her. Mrs. C. earns no income of her own and receives a monthly welfare check of $350 to provide necessary household support. Her children, aged 1 to 11, are growing and she feels she must begin work somewhere in order to earn money to buy them more clothes.

4. The family of Mr. and Mrs. D. have been living in Academy Homes since July 1965. The parents are blacks in their forties who migrated from South Carolina. They have seven children. Mr. D. is a disabled veteran and his wife remains at home to care for her family. They receive a welfare check of $300 per month. The oldest daughter will begin working soon, adding to the current income.

5. Mrs. E. is a widowed mother of six children, aged 14 to 24. A black, high-school graduate, she is unable to work because she must care for her children. She is also an asthma victim. She receives a welfare check of $332 monthly.

6. Mrs. F. is the widowed mother of five children, ages 8 to 14. Georgia bred, she came to Boston in 1947. She moved around several times due to fire and urban renewal before making her home in Academy Homes in September 1965. Displeased with her eighth grade education, she would like to return some day and become a registered nurse. At present she cannot think of school or work because she is a diabetic victim. She receives $356 per month in the form of Social Security and Veterans' Aid.

7. Mr. and Mrs. G. came to Boston from Puerto Rico in 1958 and reside in

rlame Park. Mr. G., aged 38, does not hold a continual job due to his guage barrier and total lack of education. He worked once in an auto nder factor, but soon gave up that job. Mrs. G. did receive a sixth grade ducation and sews slip covers in Brookline at $69 per week.

ey and the other thirty-three families in the rent subsidy program were alike in having little money and many children. In other respects, they varied. The one other experience they had in common was that during a fifteen-month period in 1964 and 1965 they all moved from rundown dwellings in or around the ghetto to brand new apartments in the same general section of the city.

The New Dwellings

The subsidized apartments were in three new 221 (d) (3) developments: Marksdale Gardens, Charlame Park Homes, and Academy Homes. A local church, St. Mark Congregational Church, organized and backed the development corporation which financed Marksdale. Associated Architect and Engineer, a local firm, designed it. The Development Corporation of America did the developing, building, and managing. Marksdale's site lay at the very center of the urban renewal area; the buildings went up in the midst of blocks of cleared land. The basic design set row houses with small private yards, front and back, around irregular courts. The back yards were fenced from the surrounding street. Its first two adjacent divisions, into which fourteen families from the rent supplementation program moved, contained 166 apartments.

The second new development, Charlame Park Homes, went up across the street from Marksdale. Its name represents the sponsor, Charles Street A.M.E. Church. Harold Michelson and Sumner Marcus developed and managed it, Bedar and Alpars designed it, Gardner Construction and the Lamont Corporation built it. Its two-story row houses stand back separated by small yards, along parallel streets, with a few three-story blocks among them. Altogether, there are 92 units.

About a half mile away, on a major thoroughfare which at the time set a rough western boundary to the ghetto, a Building Service Employees International Union local sponsored the construction of Academy Homes. As in Marksdale, Development Corporation of America handled building and management. Carl Koch designed it. Academy is larger than Charlame or Marksdale with 202 units. In contrast to the separate-entry two- and three-story row houses of Charlame and Marksdale, Academy consists of a combination of row houses with three- and four-story common-entry apartments, many of them set around closed squares.

The earlier stripping of vegetation from the site and the continuation of construction through much of the period of our study made the buildings of

Academy, Charlame, and Marksdale look rather bare and foreign to their surroundings. Still the three developments contained some of the most attractive housing available at any price in or around Boston's ghetto. As we shall see in detail later on, the middle-income and rent subsidy families alike generally rated their new dwellings as much superior to their previous housing.

Not that the tenants found nothing to complain about. The long shortage of grass and the consequent surplus of mud and dust in all three developments agitated many of the housewives. A number of the same women, especially those with small children, disliked the extensive use of white paint and white tile in walls and floors. Garbage storage and removal came to be worrisome issues in all three places. And some of the complaints touched the designs of the developments and the quality of construction more directly: too little, and insufficiently segregated, play space for children; paper-thin walls; inadequate laundry facilities.

One paradox struck us. Academy Homes had received several national citations for good design. Yet among our respondents, more of the complaints about design came from the tenants in Academy. Most of the dissatisfaction had to do with common spaces: entries, passages, and stairways. Academy apartment residents (who ordinarily shared their entries with four other families) complained that no one took responsibility for the upkeep of the common spaces, and they therefore tended to become run down. Most likely several other Academy residents who disliked having only a single entry to their apartments had related problems in mind. A visitor to Academy in 1965 or 1966 could see the difference between the well-tended areas outside the row-house entries and the bare patches by the multiple-entry units. The units of Marksdale and Charlame were laid out more like single-family houses, with separate entries and no common spaces. The residents of Marksdale and Charlame, in fact, regularly identified that as one of the virtues of their developments. When in our follow-up interviews we asked residents of the three areas their impressions of public housing, furthermore, they repeatedly mentioned the "lack of privacy," the "cramped quarters," and the "people living one on top of another."

While there are obviously other elements involved, the most consistent theme in all these complaints and comparisons appears to be a decided preference for each household's having a clearly bounded private space including entries and outside areas for work and storage of material belonging to the household. Where the households had even a modicum of such space, as in Marksdale and Charlame, they had room to maneuver, could control their interactions with their neighbors more effectively, retained a choice in the use and decoration of the exteriors of their homes, and knew who was responsible for the maintenance of which area. The less amount and more ambiguous character of private outside space in Academy offset to some extent what the residents recognized as other excellent features of the design.

The net effect was roughly to equalize the satisfaction of the residents of the three developments with their new dwellings. One of our standard questions asked for a comparison between the family's present and previous dwelling in terms of character and neighborhood (see Table 6-4 for details). From this inventory we derived a "preference score" running from −14 to 0 to 14, simply by assigning 1 to "like it better," −1 to "don't like it as much" and 0 to "not much difference." We shall analyze its variations among the major housing groups later. For the women we interviewed at length in Charlame, Academy, and Marksdale, the mean preference scores were:

Development	Mean Preference Score
Charlame	+4.5
Academy	+4.8
Marksdale	+5.9
Total	+5.2

Our later follow-up interviews showed the residents of the three developments to be even closer together, and in nearly unanimous agreement on the superiority of their present housing to what they had lived in before (generally private housing in the ghetto).

In each development, families receiving rent subsidies occupied about one apartment in eleven: 14 of 166 in Marksdale, 8 of 92 in Charlame, and 18 of 202 in Academy. The Boston Housing Authority arranged for them to be spread widely among families not involved in the rent subsidy program. Because families in the program had many children, however, they clustered in the larger apartments, which in Charlame and Academy were generally concentrated in certain blocks. In one section of Academy, furthermore, the Boston Housing Authority's delay in placing tenants in the rent subsidy program led to the settlement of four families in the last available apartments of a single block.

Even that concentration does not seem to have singled out the rent subsidy recipients as a group. In the last follow-up survey, our interviewers talked with fourteen of the housewives in that block.[b] Of them thirteen expressed approval of the rent subsidy principle (the fourteenth did not venture an opinion). Only *two* of the four women receiving rent subsidy payments said they knew anyone else in the program. Of the other ten women, none could identify *anyone* involved in the program. The proportion of subsidy families to others was low enough for them to melt unobtrusively into the crowd.

The Boston program, then, adds up to a modest but nonetheless remarkable social experiment. The families involved faced very important changes in some phases of their life, while maintaining continuity in most other respects. The fact that other very similar families were moving into rather different kinds of housing at about the same time makes it possible to put the changes experienced by the subsidy families in perspective. Most members of all our housing groups

---

[b]We shall discuss these interviews and this issue at greater length in a later chapter.

moved from in or around Boston's ghetto to somewhere else in the same area. The net effect was probably a very *slight* desegregation. However, the subsidy families came most exclusively from the ghetto, while their new middle-income families generally had a little more experience with racially-integrated living.

Middle-income and subsidy families alike moved into attractive, newly built row houses and apartments. Almost all of them saw the new housing as distinctly superior to what they had occupied before. The really large change, obviously, was the one the subsidy families went through. As poor families with many children, they had seen the worst of the Boston housing market. Now they moved into brand-new dwellings renting for far more than their incomes would ordinarily have permitted. More than nine-tenths of their neighbors had better jobs and more education. So the subsidy families experienced two abrupt changes: to distinctly better housing, and to neighborhoods of significantly higher social standing. One of our chief jobs in the following chapters is to examine the impact of those changes.

6

The Impact of the Program on the People

What Was the Program?

Much of what we have described as the experimental subsidy program was out of sight, invisible to any particular person involved in it. We can examine its impact in several different ways. First comes the perspective of the families receiving rent subsidies: the way they feel about the program, the way they understand it, the kinds of contacts they have with their neighbors and with the people who run the program. Then there is the observable change in their lives, if any, which can be attributed to the program. Finally there is the effect on people and things outside the program itself: the neighbors, the housing market, the pattern of segregation in the city. This chapter and the next will explore the first two sorts of impact. Chapter 8 will deal mainly with the third. Here we shall give our greatest attention to the experiences of the poor families receiving rent subsidies, try to get at the special flavor of the experience by comparing them closely with the similar families moving into public housing, and then occasionally look at all five of our housing groups.

Just what is "the program," as people actually receiving rent subsidies see it? Surprisingly few of the subsidy tenants had more than a vague idea of the program, even though month in and month out a portion of their rent was paid from the federal treasury. In the final round of interviews, conducted about six months after the last tenant had moved into a middle-income project, only a few of the twenty-nine recipients of subsidies we interviewed recognized the bureaucratic labels "rent supplementation" or "rent subsidy." Blank or puzzled looks were the rule when interviewers asked the following question:

> What do you think about the rent-subsidy method of making decent housing available for low-income families? Do you think it is a good idea?

Only *detailed* explanations of the subsidy program removed the puzzled expressions from the faces of most of the people in the program. Even then no less than six of the twenty-nine said they had had *no* personal experience with the rent-aid program. Interviewers probed extensively in several of these cases; they reported that in at least two of the six cases the respondents clearly did not know they were receiving rent subsidies. We were unable to ascertain whether the other four respondents also were ignorant of their participation in the program; they may have been withholding information. However, given the other information we have on these respondents, this seems fairly unlikely.

Moreover, many of those who admitted participation in the program seemed to be confused about it. Some were even unclear as to which agency of the government was responsible for the rent aid; for example, one respondent incorrectly reported that "We pay part and the BRA [Boston Redevelopment Authority] pays the rest." Others did not realize there was a time limit to the program. Why this haze of misunderstanding? One possible explanation is the way the rent subsidy recipients were handled. The head of the Public Housing Authority at the time informed us that the PHA did not tell the subsidy families too much at the early stage because they did not want the program advertised publicly before they made a formal public announcement. Yet even well into the program many of the recipients were still misinformed. Another explanation lies in the handling of the subsidy payments themselves. The project administration actually received the federal payment, a check sent through the Boston Housing Authority; all the tenant saw was a lower rent figure. After several months, or years, of paying this lower figure, she may have forgotten (even if she once knew) that she was receiving a direct rent subsidy at all. Doubtless this haze of misunderstanding and misinformation is not unique to the Boston program. It seems to be characteristic of many contacts low-income persons have with both public and private bureaucracies.

Among those who were aware they were receiving rent subsidies there was general enthusiasm for the program. The following are typical comments from the follow-up interviews:

"I think it's a good idea. It's been a big help."

"There should be more. Gives a chance for us to live as we rightfully should."

"It helps you a lot to know that you can live happy and decent like one who can really afford it."

"It's wonderful. I agree 100 percent."

"It gives poor people a chance to live in a decent place."

"I would like to see it continued forever."

Moreover, when they were asked if they would like to continue to participate beyond the time limit of the program, not one of the twenty-three who admitted personal experience with the program made negative comments about the rent subsidy; and all said they would like to continue receiving a subsidy at least for a while.[a] Admittedly some qualified this by saing that they wanted to get off the subsidy program as soon as they could afford it. This was not because of any specific criticisms of the program but rather because they shared the general American values of independence and self-reliance. Typical comments in this regard are illustrative:

"I like to do right; I don't like to slip by on nothing."

"Re-examination will yield some denial of the program. If I'm not eligible, I'm ready to give it up. . . . People feel better, at least, I do, if they are self-supporting."

"Yes. I would like to continue on it until my husband can get a better paying job."

"I would like to be able to get off it."

Our general feeling is that almost all, if not all, of the subsidy recipients were very glad they received this rent aid. But it is also our impression that most would like to be self-supporting and planned to get off the program as soon as they were financially able. Contrary to the suggestions of certain critics of the subsidy idea, this program and similar programs will probably not make most recipients permanent wards of the government.

Stigma?

In a January 24, 1966, article, Stanley Penn of *The Wall Street Journal* made the following comment about Boston's rent subsidy program:

A middle-aged Negro woman who lives in a comfortable four-bedroom apartment on the city's southwest side has a secret she closely guards from her neighbors—Uncle Sam pays $54 of her monthly rent.

This article raises important questions about the impact of the subsidy program on the recipients. Did they feel stigmatized by the other residents? Did anyone else in the project know they were receiving a subsidy? Did it make any difference to them? Did they feel the need to keep the subsidy an iron-clad secret? The fact that many of the recipients themselves had only a vague conception of the subsidy program leads one to predict "no" answers to such questions.

---

[a]Although it was not intended by us, the "time limit" phrase in our questions surprised some of the respondents. One said: "They didn't give me a limit." This is further evidence of the haze of misunderstanding.

Of the twenty-three tenants who knew (or admitted) they were receiving a rent subsidy, only six definitely indicated that they felt other residents of the middle-income projects *knew* about the subsidy. One other respondent said she just didn't know. The others, 70 percent of the total, reported that as far as they knew other residents were not aware of the subsidy they received. Of the six who reported that other tenants knew about the subsidy, only one also said "yes" to the additional question, "Do you think it makes any difference to them?" The reason for this seems to be that the few other residents who did know about the rent subsidies were, as one respondent put it, "doing the same thing or would like to do the same thing."

Of the seventeen respondents who indicated that other residents did *not* know about their rent subsidy, only one indicated that it would definitely make a difference to the other tenants if they knew. As she phrased it, "People have a way of being quite snobbish about it." One other respondent said "maybe yes"; and a few others were uncertain as to whether it would make any difference to other residents if they knew. As far as we could tell from our interviews, at most only a few of our respondents might fit the view of Mr. Penn, that is, a subsidy tenant carefully guarding her identity from her neighbors.[b]

Of course, some might suggest that the subsidy tenants were stigmatized by the other tenants; they were just unaware of it. This suggestion is on the face of it improbable. Evidence from the thirty-two interviews with nonsubsidy, middle-income tenants of the same projects also does not jibe with this suggestion. In spite of the fact that they were substantially better-off financially than the subsidy tenants, they too were overwhelmingly in favor of rent subsidies for low-income families. (It should be noted that most of them also did not know the meaning of the specific term "rent subsidy.") Only *one* of the middle-income respondents expressed strong negative feelings about a subsidization approach. She said that "it takes responsibility away from the individual." But even she had mixed feelings, adding, "Maybe some people could benefit by it." A few others qualified their endorsement of a rent subsidy approach, but the overwhelming majority thought it was a good idea and attached no stigma to those who might receive subsidies. "It gives poor people a chance for better housing."

A related question we asked also bears on this issue of stigmatization. Officials in one of the developments had said that three of the subsidy families were giving the project a bad name and that some of the middle-income tenants were ready to leave because they feared (and knew) their subsidized neighbors.

[b]The interviewer who completed most of the interviews with the subsidy families made the following suggestive contrast between the subsidy program and ordinary welfare programs: "I felt that the subsidy tenants who were on ADC placed ADC payments and subsidy in entirely different categories. Subsidy was in no way considered "welfare" and had no social stigma attached to it. Perhaps this is due to the fact that there were many families with mother and father present receiving a subsidy—making the female family head less singled out."

We found no evidence of this. In the process of a probing interview only two of the thirty-two middle-income tenants (including twelve living *next door* to subsidy recipients) reported that they knew someone receiving a rent subsidy. One thought her cousin was receiving rent aid; another said a friend was receiving a subsidy. In addition to these two respondents three others—two in Academy Homes—felt that there were subsidy tenants in their projects. This vague awareness may well have been a result—not a cause—of the administrative discontent with the subsidy families in Academy Homes. The assumption that the middle-income tenants would leave (or were about to leave) because of the low-income tenants was also without foundation. Of the thirty-two wives interviewed only five said "no" to the questions: "Do you expect to be living here five years from now?" And of these five *not one* was also a respondent who knew a subsidy recipient or who suspected there were subsidy recipients in their development. The reasons they gave for moving were connected with the ideal of home ownership. No one, including four others vaguely considering a move, said they planned to move because of the presence of low-income or rent subsidy families.[c]

The Housing Itself

We have already described the three new developments into which the families receiving direct rent subsidies moved. We have not yet laid out in hard numbers how the housing change those forty families experienced compared with that of families entering public housing or the private market.

In almost all respects, the subsidy families experienced a greater change for the better than the members of the other housing groups. In terms of median number of rooms occupied, for example, the before/after comparison goes like this:

	Before	After
Nonmovers	5.0	5.0
Private	5.5	6.0
Public	5.0	5.0
Subsidy	5.0	7.0
Middle Income	6.0	6.0

---

[c]One additional question is in order at this point. Were the subsidy tenants themselves aware of other such tenants in the same housing development? Over half of the twenty-nine subsidy recipients interviewed said they did not know or know about other subsidy tenants. And several of those who replied "yes" to the question, "Do you know anyone else (in the development) who has received a rent subsidy?" were only dimly aware that "someone else" was receiving a rent subsidy too. One said, "I know there are more here but I've never met any of them"; another commented, "There are seven of us. A social worker from the BRA told me; I don't know who's who."

While those finding their own housing in the private market also increased the size of their dwellings dramatically, the subsidy families averaged two full rooms more than they had before. What is more, the increased space was all in new, sound, attractive dwellings.

To be sure, they paid more for that space. The median monthly rent (not total housing cost) for the different categories was:

	Nonmover	Private	Public	Subsidy[a]	Middle Income
Before	54.00	62.50	62.50	55.00	70.00
After	54.00	65.00	65.00	70.00	109.00
Change	0	+2.50	+2.50	+15.00	+29.00

[a]This figure does not, of course, include the subsidy paid by the Housing Authority, which averaged another $50. The fact that the total rent paid for the subsidy families' apartments is larger than the middle-income total results from the larger dwellings occupied by the subsidy families, which in turn is due to their larger average number of children.

The rent paid by the nonmovers stayed the same. The people moving in the private market or into public housing paid a bit more, on the average, the subsidy and middle-income families paid heftier rents after the move, even though the subsidy families were having part of the way paid by the federal government. (See Table 6-1.) And in fact, the comments made by the women we interviewed underlined this difference: the public housing families generally felt that the rent paid was one of the best features of the new housing, while the subsidy families generally felt it was one of the worst. Over the whole sample, the net effect of the move was to shift people from rents under $65 per month toward rents of $70 and more per month. Nowhere was this more dramatic than in the middle-income families. They began with almost three-quarters paying rent under $90, and ended with almost everyone paying rents over $90. The subsidy families also shifted upwards, although not as much. Only two or three of the private families moved into the high-rent categories and the move into public housing actually meant a slight decrease in the number paying high rents. In terms of rent paid, then, the public families did better than the subsidy families.

How much did these rent payments cut into their incomes? We face some difficulties in calculating reliable rent-income ratios. Many families in several of the categories were receiving important parts of their incomes from public agencies, especially through Aid to Families with Dependent Children. At the time of our initial interviews, for example, the proportions getting *all* their reported income from public agencies were:

Nonmovers	44%
Private	12
Public	21

Subsidy	17
Middle Income	7
Total	18%

Even more had erratic sources of income, like seasonal jobs. As a result, it was hard to assemble a completely accurate estimate of their yearly incomes. In general, the women gave slightly lower estimates of their income after the move than before:

Median Stated Income for Previous Year

	Before	After
Nonmovers	$4000	$3150
Private	4250	4200
Public	3000	2950
Subsidy	4000	3600
Middle	5500	4200

Table 6-1
Changes in Rents Paid Before and After Moving

Before Move: Percentage of Each Category

	Nonmover	Private	Public	Subsidy	Middle Income	Total
Number	16	16	24	35	29	120
Monthly Rent						
No answer	12%	12%	0%	0%	3%	4%
$1-$65	50	56	62	71	31	55
$66-$90	31	31	29	26	41	32
$91-$105	6	0	4	3	17	7
over $105	0	0	4	0	7	2
Total	99%	99%	99%	100%	99%	100%

After Move: Percentage of Each Category

	Nonmover	Private	Public	Subsidy	Middle Income	Total
Number	16	16	24	35	29	120
Monthly Rent						
No answer	6%	19%	0%	0%	0%	3%
$1-$65	56	38	71	43	0	39
$66-$90	31	31	25	34	3	24
$91-$105	0	12	4	20	31	16
over $105	6	0	0	3	66	17
Total	99%	100%	100%	100%	100%	99%

Although a bit surprising, these figures are not impossible; in most cases, the women did outline their income in some detail, and in most cases two different years are involved. Nevertheless, they raise enough suspicions (particularly in the case of the middle-income families) that we have calculated rent-income ratios twice: once using the respondents' own reports of family income, a second time using the Boston Housing Authority's and Boston Redevelopment Authority's estimates of their income.[d] Table 6-2 gives the breakdowns based on the families' own reports of their income. Again, the subsidy and middle-income families appear to have borne the brunt of the increase in rent. But now it also looks as though they may have been the best prepared to bear it. By these reports, the middle-income families were sacrificing most financially by moving. Most of them went from paying under 20 percent to paying over 25 percent of their incomes for rent. That change is due less to the rise in rent than to the fall in the incomes they reported. Even with the substantial increase, the subsidy families ended up paying a somewhat smaller proportion of their income for rent than the families moving into public housing or private housing. (The apparent decline for the nonmovers may be because the Redevelopment Authority took over a few of the dwellings in question in anticipation of razing them, and set lower rents for them; in any case, this was not permanent.) The increases are, of course, aggravated by the fact that the families reported lower incomes after the move.

We can estimate the same change more conservatively by using the administratively-determined family incomes both before and after the move. This is shown in Table 6-3. Since the rent figures are the same in the two sets of tables, the differences between the two sets come solely from the discrepancies between "administrative" income and the income the families reported to our interviewers. The new calculations still show a rise in rent-income ratios for every group but the nonmovers. The middle-income families still appear to have made the largest jump, but not so large as before.

Both ways of analyzing the change, nevertheless, identify the same pattern of relative advantage. Perhaps we can best sum it up in terms of *change* in the median percentage of income spent on rent:

	Nonmover	Private	Public	Subsidy	Middle Income	Total
Using stated income	−1.2	2.8	1.1	3.7	12.3	4.9
Using administrative	−1.9	2.1	1.9	2.2	8.2	3.1

[d]This second calculation obviously involves assuming no change in income over the time of the study, which would lead to an underestimate of post-move ratios if there actually was a decline in income. We have, incidentally, used contract rent instead of rent plus heat and utilities because in a number of the post-move interviews the women we talked to were not yet sure what these additional costs were going to come to.

Table 6-2
Families' Own Reports of Income

| | Before Move: Percentage of Each Category | | | | | |
	Nonmover	Private	Public	Subsidy	Middle Income	Total
Number	16	16	24	35	29	120
Percentage of income paid for rent						
Not available	12	12	8	6	10	9
1-15%	25	12	12	40	34	28
16-20	19	38	21	20	34	26
21-25	25	25	21	20	10	19
26-30	19	6	12	9	3	9
over 30	0	6	25	6	7	9
Median percentage of income	20.0	19.2	22.9	16.2	16.0	18.1

| | After Move: Percentage of Each Category | | | | | |
	Nonmover	Private	Public	Subsidy	Middle Income	Total
Number	16	16	24	35	29	120
Percentage of income paid for rent						
Not available	12	25	8	9	24	15
1-15%	25	25	0	3	3	8
16-20	25	0	12	43	14	22
21-25	12	31	42	17	7	21
26-30	19	6	17	11	21	15
over 30	6	12	21	17	31	19
Median percentage of income	18.8	22.0	24.0	19.9	28.3	23.0

At this general level, the only important discrepancy appears in the figures for middle-income families. Both calculations show the families who move into public housing experiencing less of an increase than those receiving direct rent subsidies. Nevertheless, both calculations also show that the public housing families end up worst off of all the low-income categories in this respect, because they began by paying so much of their meager incomes for rent. The changes for the private and subsidy groups resembled each other. In line with the common experience of people displaced by urban renewal, most families ended up paying *higher* rents after the move, and the subsidy families' experience was not much different from the others. Where they differed was in what they got for the increased outlay.

Table 6-3
Administratively Determined Reports of Income

| | Before Move: Percentage of Each Category | | | | | |
	Nonmover	Private	Public	Subsidy	Middle Income	Total
Number	16	16	24	35	29	120
Percentage of income paid for rent						
Not available	12	12	0	0	3	4
1-15%	31	31	8	43	41	32
16-20	12	19	17	29	21	21
21-25	19	31	17	23	17	21
26-30	12	0	25	3	14	11
over 30	12	6	33	3	3	11
Median percentage of income	20.4	19.0	25.4	16.9	17.5	19.0

| | After Move: Percentage of Each Category | | | | | |
	Nonmover	Private	Public	Subsidy	Middle Income	Total
Number	16	16	24	35	29	120
Percentage of income paid for rent						
Not available	6	19	0	0	0	3
1-15%	44	12	4	0	3	9
16-20	6	19	8	66	17	28
21-25	12	38	25	14	24	22
26-30	19	6	33	6	28	18
over 30	12	6	29	14	28	19
Median percentage of income	18.5	21.1	26.3	19.1	25.7	22.1

Satisfaction with the New Environment

This section will examine several issues related to the central question of satisfaction. Just how satisfied were the rent subsidy families with their new housing environment?

This and subsequent sections dealing with the impact of the program on the people will emphasize the data on the thirty-five black subsidy families and on twenty-four black public housing families—all very poor families by American standards. This latter group is in many ways the most important comparison group, since both these groups were "handled" by the Boston Housing Authority and both groups were probably destined for public housing at the outset. In fact, the subsidy families had to qualify for public housing. Moreover, as noted in an earlier chapter, the national debate on rent supplements has frequently seen this "new" program contrasted with the existing public housing program.

In the previous chapter we briefly touched on the finding that our 221 (d) (3) families saw their move as generally improving their circumstances. They were generally satisfied with their new facilities. This also applies to the subsidy tenants taken by themselves, as can be seen in Table 6-4.

Looking at the subsidy columns, it is clear that on almost every item the proportion liking their 221 (d) (3) apartment better than the last place they lived far exceeds the proportion not liking it as much as the last place. This is particularly true of the important items bearing on the space, design, safety, quietness, and childrearing features of the 221 (d) (3) environment. In each case the percentage "liking it better" is between 83 and 94 percent. And in each case the "like better-don't like as much" differential and the absolute percentage are greater than the comparable figures for the public housing sample, although

Table 6-4
Comparison of Present and Previous Residence, After the Move

	Subsidy (N=35)		Public (N=24)	
Compared to the last place you lived, do you like x better, worse, or the same	Percentage Replying "Like it Better"	Percentage Replying "Don't like it as much"	Percentage Replying "Like it Better"	Percentage Replying "Don't like it as much"
The size of this place	91	3	75	4
The outside of the building	94	3	75	13
The amount of rent you pay	66	26	96	4
Amount of space you have to invite friends over	91	6	67	8
Amount of space you have to be by yourself when you want	91	6	58	8
As a place to bring up children	83	3	58	17
Grocery stores	31	46	29	50
Nearness to public transp.	60	20	42	25
Nearness to your church	29	43	13	54
Places for entertainment[a]	20	20	13	50
Schools[a]	40	26	33	17
Class of people who live near	46	3	21	25
The safety of the street	83	9	63	21
The quietness of the street	86	9	29	46

[a]A substantial percentage of answers were in the "can't say" (NA) category.

those figures also indicate in most cases satisfaction with the new public housing environment.

On the issues of rent and nearness to public transportation, the proportion of the population "liking them better" is large (over 60 percent), although not as large as for the features noted above. It should be noted that 20 to 26 percent of the sample were dissatisfied with the 221 (d) (3) situation in each respect. In regard to rent it is clear that a larger proportion of the subsidy sample were dissatisfied than of the public housing sample. Ninety-six percent of the public housing group liked the rent they now paid.

We find somewhat less enthusiasm for the other features of the new neighborhoods. On the whole, people felt the schools and "the class of people" in the new area were better. But more people replied "don't like it as much" than replied "like it better" when it came to grocery stores and nearness to church. Many families had moved inconveniently far from their neighborhood churches, and at the time of the interviewing the area around two of the 221 (d) (3) developments was almost entirely razed for renewal. Since then, local stores have opened up, and the complaints have probably gone down.

In sum, on eleven of the fourteen features of the dwelling area our interviewers asked about, the proportion of our rent subsidy respondents preferring the new environment exceeded the proportion preferring the old. In most cases the great majority prefer the new place.[e] When compared to the public housing sample as a group, the subsidy respondents appear much more satisfied with the move they have made. One simple datum makes the point very well. When we asked how much they liked this place they were living in, 83 percent of the subsidy respondents said "very much." For tenants in public housing, the proportion was only 29 percent.

If we take the fourteen items we have compared and assign a score of +1 for each answer of "like it better," 0 for each answer of "like it the same" and −1 for each answer of "don't like it as much," we can sum to arrive at a Satisfaction Score running from −14 (everything about the new dwelling is worse than the old one) to +14 (everything about the new dwelling is better) with a midpoint of 0 (as many things better as worse). Since we asked this question both before the move and after, the first comparison dealing with the dwelling occupied at the time of the first interview and the dwelling before *that*, we have an opportunity to check whether the differences among the groups simply represent differences in optimism. They do not. The mean Satisfaction Scores were:

---

[e]To add another item, 17 percent of the subsidy respondents, as compared with 33 percent of the public housing respondents, reported that something had gone wrong with their apartment in the last few months. When asked how much the landlord did when things went wrong, 6 percent of the subsidy respondents, as compared with 13 percent of the public housing respondents, said the landlord did "little or nothing."

	Before	After
Nonmover	+4.9	+2.8
Private	+2.3	+3.2
Public	+1.3	+2.7
Subsidy	+2.7	+6.4
Middle Income	+4.2	+4.3

The nonmovers, who were still comparing the same dwellings the second time, grew less enthusiastic as their neighborhoods were torn down around them. All other groups saw the last move as an improvement, the public housing families least, the subsidy families most.

Another way of getting at this comparison is to see what people said when asked general questions about dwelling and neighborhood:

What do you think most people would say about the way this neighborhood looks in general? Would they call it very nice, fairly nice, nothing special, fairly bad, or very bad?

What do you think most people would say about the way this building looks on the outside?

Would you say you like this place very much, fairly well, all right, not too well, or not at all?

We can tabulate the most negative answers to the questions this way:

	Percentage Calling Neighborhood "very bad"		Percentage Calling Building "very bad"		Percentage Liking this place "not at all"	
	Before	After	Before	After	Before	After
Nonmover	19	6	6	12	12	6
Private	50	6	44	0	31	0
Public	17	0	25	4	17	12
Subsidy	29	0	29	0	29	0
Middle income	21	0	17	3	17	0

There are some minor inconsistencies between these items and the Satisfaction Scores, but on the whole the message is the same: most people in all groups preferred the new location to the old. Here at the negative end of the opinion range, the tenants of public housing still appear less satisfied than the rest. Virtually none of the people in the subsidy, private, or middle-income categories give their new dwellings or neighborhoods really bad marks.

The difference in experience had an interesting effect on people's attitudes toward urban renewal. We asked two questions about renewal:

In general, would you say that this area is better off because of urban renewal, worse off because of it, or that it really doesn't make much difference? (Asked both before and after move)

Do you feel that the urban renewal has helped you personally? (Asked after move only).

Let us tabulate the answers in the usual way:

	Percentage Saying Area Is "Better Off" Through Renewal		Percentage Saying Urban Renewal Has Helped Them
	Before	After	After
Nonmover	69	25	19
Private	50	31	38
Public	54	30	4
Subsidy	69	97	80
Middle income	76	90	76

We must remember that all but the nonmovers were talking about different areas at the two interviews. Clearly the families moving into the new 221 (d) (3) developments not only saw a connection between their own experiences and the whole renewal program but also found their own part of it a considerable success. Meanwhile, the public, private, and especially nonmover families were growing more sour about renewal. The experience with relocation colored a much wider range of attitudes.

The Daily Routine

Moving meant rearranging the daily round of activities temporarily or permanently. We attempted to get at the changes in daily routine by employing a time budget. The basic question (and the accompanying instructions to the interviewer) went like this:

W10a. Now I'd like to get a picture of your activities on weekdays, say yesterday. (Note to interviewer: If "Yesterday is actually a Saturday or a Sunday, say "Friday." Do *not* get a time budget for Saturday or Sunday.) What were you doing at 6 in the morning? Until when? Where were you? Who was with you? What did you do next? Until when? Where? Who was with you? (Note to interviewer: Continue until 12 midnight: If respondent names two activities at once, list the second(ary) activity in the secondary column.)

Social setting for *each* fifteen-minute period. If activity, location, or social setting is continued from one fifteen-minute period to the next, indicate by drawing vertical continuation lines. Coders should not be forced to guess what was happening.

Unfortunately for comparability, we and our interviewers became much more skilled at collecting time budgets as we completed the first round of interviews. In that first round, for example, our interviewers left an average of 27 minutes per day simply unrecorded, while in the postmove interviews the average was only 8 minutes. Furthermore, we learned to press harder for details when a woman reported she had done "housework" from 9 A.M. to 4 P.M. or was "taking care of the children" all evening.

For these reasons, we have more confidence in the postmove reports than in those collected before the move, and are certain that some of the apparent changes at the time of the move result from the improvement in our recording. Nevertheless, the improvements in recording occurred across the board. If one group changed more than the others, or in another direction, we have some reason for paying attention to it.

The analysis of these time budgets has turned out to be cumbersome (the data presented in the next few tables are contained in about 24,000 punched cards) and intricate (the data reported here represent only the simplest condensation of only one variable within a whole web of observations on multiple activities, locations, social settings, and so on). It has taken us two years to develop a system for flexible handling of data of this volume and complexity. The data we have to offer here deal, for technical reasons, with a larger sample of 162 women (white and black). They describe the principal activities these women reported carrying out between 6 A.M. and midnight. We would guess from the reports that the average woman in the sample spent another 350 minutes sleeping between midnight and 6 A.M. It does not describe secondary activities like watching television while cleaning house, although our records do catch many such activities. The tables themselves present the mean numbers of *minutes* reported for each of nine large categories of activity, plus the mean numbers of minutes unspecified.

These were the reports (in minutes) from the before-move interviews. Before the move, the allocations of time in the different groups resembled each other very greatly. Overall, the most similar pairs were middle income/private, public/subsidy, and public/nonmover. The least alike were public/private and subsidy/middle income. The last one is interesting because those two groups were to become neighbors. But one of the differences was enormous. The largest variable element was the time spent working outside the home. The middle-income women averaged three times as much work time outside the home as the subsidy women. Since these are averages, what this really means is that about

Activity	Private N=17	Public N=31	Subsidy N=40	Middle Income N=50	Nonmover N=24	Total N=162
Unspecified	28	21	38	18	33	27
Care for self and others	135	187	193	150	162	168
Housekeeping	135	178	131	131	147	143
Eating and cooking	234	201	229	201	201	212
Sleeping	132	150	136	134	159	141
Recreation	254	235	245	238	212	237
Travel	29	22	25	31	18	26
Commercial	17	16	33	21	36	25
Work	107	70	51	157	102	100
Other	9	1	0	1	10	3
Total	1080	1081	1081	1082	1080	1082

one woman in three in the middle-income group, as compared with only one woman in eight or nine in the subsidy group, was away at work most of the day.

After the move, the reports looked like this:

Activity	Private N=17	Public N=31	Subsidy N=40	Middle Income N=50	Nonmover N=24	Total N=162
Unspecified	7	13	5	4	14	8
Care for self and others	116	129	176	159	126	148
Housekeeping	91	205	235	150	125	172
Eating and cooking	228	248	237	184	179	213
Sleeping	152	118	125	124	149	130
Recreation	240	287	221	213	267	240
Travel	30	15	16	36	30	26
Commercial	45	16	15	25	57	28
Work	154	44	41	183	112	108
Other	17	4	9	3	19	9
Total	1080	1079	1080	1081	1078	1082

Our greater experience with this sort of interviewing greatly reduced the time unaccounted for. Otherwise, it did not affect the reported allocation of time for the sample as a whole very much. The move, which took the families from relatively similar to relatively dissimilar neighborhoods, does seem to have the expected effect: the time budgets of the various groups differ much more after the move than before. The public/subsidy and nonmover/private pairs are now most alike, the private/subsidy and nonmover/subsidy most unlike each other. But the pattern of differences remains the same. Time spent at work outside the home is still the most variable item.

We can identify the changes from before to after the move a little more clearly by computing the ratio between the time spent on any particular activity after the move and the time spent on that activity before the move. If the mean time spent traveling after the move was 30 minutes, and the mean time before the move 20 minutes, the ratio will be 30/20 = 1.5. Values below 1 will indicate a reduction in the time spent on that activity, values above 1 an increase, and values around 1 no change. The table to follow also includes an Index of Dissimilarity between the distribution of time before and after the move. It can be interpreted approximately as the proportion of all the time in one of the distributions which would have to be reallocated in order to make it exactly the same as the other distribution. For example, it might take a reduction of 10 minutes sleeping time and 20 minutes housekeeping time, plus an increase of 30 minutes work time to make the after-move time budget the same as the before-move budget; a reallocation of 30 minutes would do it. That index reads 0 for identical distributions, 100 for absolutely different ones.

Even though each group had a somewhat different pattern, in general people hold on to the time allocations they were already used to. The daily routines of the public and subsidy families (who were, in fact, making the largest changes in location and type of dwelling) apparently changed the most. The middle-income families stayed closest to their previous patterns.

The overall decreases in unspecified activities and increases in "other" activities come, as we have said, from the improvements in our interviewing procedure. Quite likely some of the apparent increase in housekeeping activity is because our interviewers probed more carefully in the second interview. It does look, however, as though the subsidy women's complaints about the difficulties of keeping white-tiled kitchens and grassless yards clean had some basis in their

Table 6-5
Before and After the Move Ratios of Time Spent on Daily Activities

Activity	Private	Public	Subsidy	Middle Income	Nonmover	Total
Unspecified	0.3	0.6	0.1	0.2	0.4	0.3
Care for self and others	0.9	0.7	0.9	1.1	0.8	0.9
Housekeeping	0.7	1.2	1.7	1.2	0.8	1.2
Eating and cooking	1.0	1.2	1.0	0.9	0.9	1.0
Sleeping	1.2	0.8	0.9	0.9	0.9	0.9
Recreation	0.9	1.2	0.9	0.9	1.3	1.0
Travel	1.0	0.7	0.6	1.1	1.6	1.0
Commercial	2.6	1.0	0.4	1.2	1.6	1.1
Work	1.4	0.6	0.8	1.2	1.1	1.1
Other	0.5	4.0	–	3.0	2.0	2.7
Total	1.0	1.0	1.0	1.0	1.0	1.0
Index of Dissimilarity before/after	9.8	12.0	11.2	6.0	10.0	4.7

own experience. They reported much more time for sweeping and scrubbing after the move. Their middle-income neighbors, however, changed little with the move, and ended up spending much less time at housekeeping than the subsidy women did. The only other substantial changes shown in the table are in the time spent on travel and commercial activity (which means shopping, most of all). With only these crude data at hand, we have no way of checking out several different possible explanations for those changes.

We expect the data on the sequence and social setting of these various activities, when they become available, to show rather greater changes in the daily pattern, especially for the public and subsidy families. For the time being, we must rely on other kinds of information for some sense of how the move affected the social lives of the different groups. The next chapter will deal with that issue.

7

Social Life With and Without Rent Subsidies

Observers of American cities have formed conflicting ideas of slum and ghetto areas. One tradition, summed up eloquently by Louis Wirth's "Urbanism as a Way of Life," has treated urbanization as a process of cutting and depersonalizing social bonds. And many researchers (for example, Burgess, Zorbaugh, McKenzie) have considered that the slum accentuates the worst features of urbanism—isolation, anonymity, social disorganization. In the 1950s some urban renewal administrators and downtown merchants, arguing for the demolition of slum areas, emphasized the threat of anonymity, mobility, juvenile delinquency, and crime; Herbert Gans has portrayed this line of argument very well in his discussion of renewal in Boston's West End.[1]

But there is another way to look at the slum. In *Street Corner Society*, William F. Whyte raised some serious doubts about the view of the slum as an urban jungle. Basing his analysis on observation of life in Boston's North End, Whyte argued that some slum areas are literally teeming with social life. On the basis of his research he argued that there are different types of slum areas, ranging from highly individualized rooming-house districts to highly organized immigrant ghettos. More recent studies of another "slum" area of Boston—Boston's West End—have revealed extensive and intensive, if encapsulated and localized, networks among low-income urbanites.[2]

This same continuum, from urban jungle to urban village, of slum communities is also applicable to black ghettos. Although much current research has focused on ghetto pathology, crime, juvenile delinquency, and the like, we must not overlook the question of social organization, such as friendship, kinship, and neighboring networks, in such areas. The key question is: Does not "ordinary" social life exist, even in a black ghetto, for a majority of ghetto residents?

A "yes" answer to such a question would be important for a variety of reasons. It would in part explain the facility with which information on jobs, housing aid, riots and a variety of other subjects spreads throughout the ghetto. Such networks of interpersonal relations are crucial to the communicative integration, to the extent that such exists, of most urban communities. Communication between individuals and families need not be construed only in terms of messages, opinions, or "news." Broadly conceived, communication can be seen as including the exchange of help, money, and aid between friends or relatives, the exchange of marriage partners between families, or the exchange of job favors between relatives or friends. In sociopsychological terms, interpersonal relations often provide for the exchange of affectual support and

111

emotional security. Of particular importance in the following discussion will be the role of such informal ties in the moves of low-income blacks. Since their moves were relatively short, one might initially expect such informal ties to be important before, during, and after the move.

Informal Ties

What was the extent of informal ties in the Boston ghetto? What happened to them with the move? "Neighboring" is an informal tie of great importance to most urbanites. Commenting on the phenomenon of neighboring, not a few journalists and sociologists have given the impression that it is a predominantly middle-class and suburban phenomenon. There is some empirical evidence for a gradient pattern, with the amount of neighboring increasing as one moves from central city areas to suburbia. Yet such findings should not be interpreted to mean that neighboring is of no importance in low-income areas. A few researchers have reported that a majority of their low-income respondents in "high-familistic" areas did visit with their neighbors. The data on our rent subsidy and public housing samples bear out this finding:

		Subsidy (N=35)	Public (N=24)
Percentage talking with at least one-two neighbors often	Before	80	92
	After	83	67
Percentage visiting in homes of at least one-two neighbors	Before	71	88
	After	60	67

Before the move the proportion who reported talking often with at least one or two neighbors was 80 percent in the case of the subsidy tenants and 92 percent in the case of the public housing group. The corresponding proportions after the move were 83 percent and 67 percent, a slight gain for the subsidy group and a significant decline for the public housing group. The proportion of rent subsidy recipients who reported visiting in the homes of at least one or two neighbors went down from 71 percent before the move to 60 percent after the move, the corresponding figures for the public housing group being 88 percent and 67 percent. This latter phenomenon of some drop-off for both groups was also true in regard to the number of neighbors' names known.

However we should remember that tenants in both groups have been in projects for varying lengths of time. When the two after-move groups are divided into subgroups according to time elapsed since date of move-in (a procedure admittedly problematical because of the small number in such subgroups), the pattern seems to be an initial drop-off in neighboring in the few weeks right after the move, then a *resurgence* a month or two later.[a] The resurgence was greater for the rent subsidy subgroup which had been "in" for ten weeks or more than for the corresponding public housing subgroup. Thus the general picture of neighboring seems to be as follows: a substantial majority of both groups, of low-income blacks before and after the move into improved housing, were engaged in significant neighboring behavior; not unexpectedly the effect of the move was to decrease neighboring somewhat in the first few weeks for both groups, with a resurgence shortly thereafter. Net gains in neighboring were reported by the respondents in the subsidy subgroup which had been "in" for ten weeks or more; the corresponding public housing subgroups reported minor net losses in neighboring. Responses to another question, "Do you think of this area where you live as a neighborhood?" fit in with these data. The proportion of the public housing group responding "no" went down slightly with the move (from 29 percent to 25 percent), while the proportion of the subsidy group definitely responding "no" went down from 23 percent to 0 percent.

Another informal tie of importance to most urbanites is the tie of friendship. In our interviews both before and after the move we asked our respondents to enumerate their friends, together with addresses and frequency of contact. Each friend listed was scored from zero to six depending on the frequency of contact (six = three times a week or more often). These scores were summed to give each respondent a total interaction score. The "before" mean contact scores were 8.1 for the subsidy sample and 12.1 for the public housing sample, with less than a fifth of both groups reporting *no* contact with friends. The median number of friends for both groups was two. The "after" mean scores were greater in both cases, 11.9 for the rent subsidy group and 13.0 for the public housing group. Division of both samples into subgroups according to increasing amounts of time elapsed since date of move-in reveals an erratic pattern for the public housing subgroups and a pattern of substantial net *gain* in friendship interaction (over time) for the subsidy subgroups. However the small size of the subgroups and some difficulties in getting interviewers to make complete lists of friends in the "before" round of interviews necessitate the use of caution in interpreting these gains. One crucial point is not controvertible. Most of our rent subsidy families were involved in important, if limited (two, three, or four friends) friendship networks after the move into the new middle-income projects; they do not differ significantly from the public housing group in this respect. Neither group became isolated.

---

[a]Two points need emphasis here. First, our after-move interviews come fairly soon after the moves, and thus do not tell us as much as we need to know to assess the long-run effects of mobility on social life. Second, the subdivision of respondents (in the after-move period) into time-in groups enables us crudely but inadequately to simulate the longitudinal pattern of social link change. Thus our inferences about changes with increasing time in the new housing come from *cross-sectional* comparisons.

Generally these friendship ties appeared localized and encapsulated; plotting the addresses of friends revealed that almost all were confined to the ghetto area, the Roxbury-Dorchester-South End area of Boston. Few links extended beyond the ghetto walls. We also found that interaction tended to decrease with the distance the respondent lived from a friend, indicating that proximity affects interaction even within the ghetto. This too points to the localization of intimate ties.[b]

A third informal tie on which ghetto residents lean for support is the kinship tie. Calculated on the same basis as the friendship scores, the mean kinship interaction scores were initially somewhat higher for both groups; 10.3 for the rent subsidy sample and 12.3 for the public housing sample, with 74 percent of the former and 79 percent of the latter reporting some contact with relatives in the Boston area before their moves. After the move the mean scores were somewhat less, 9.7 for both rent subsidy tenants and the public housing group, the net drop being greater for the public housing group. Division into subgroups on the basis of time elapsed since date of move-in suggests something like a dip-rise pattern; a substantial decline in interaction in the first few weeks after the move with a resurgence thereafter, but in both cases the resurgence does not quite come up to the premove level. As with friendship ties, these kin ties also appear encapsulated, limited almost entirely to the ghetto area.

Some additional data suggest the importance of these three types of primary ties during the move-in period. Each respondent was asked three questions about the number of neighbors, friends, and relatives who helped her move into her new apartment. Eleven percent of the subsidy group reported aid from neighbors, compared to one-quarter of the public housing group. Forty-three percent of the subsidy group received aid from friends, compared to 42 percent of the public housing group. Fifty-four percent of the subsidy group received aid from relatives, compared to half of the public housing group. It is evident, and expected, that these black respondents—in both groups of poor families—relied much more heavily on previous friendships and kin ties during the move-in period than they did on their new neighbors; this fits in with the previously noted dip in mean neighboring scores for those respondents "in" for just a few weeks. Such data clearly suggest the importance of informal social ties to black families in times of minor crisis such as a move, particularly ties to friends and relatives.

	Subsidy (N=35)	Public (N=24)
Percentage reporting relatives helped them move in	54	50

[b]These statements are actually based on statistics calculated for the whole group of 120 ghetto families interviewed. Our strong impression is that they apply equally as well to the subsamples.

Percentage reporting neighbors helped them move in	11	25
Percentage reporting friends helped them move in	43	42

Up to this point we have reviewed the data on informal social ties for both the rent subsidy sample and the public housing sample. The general picture developed would seem to be as follows: most of these black respondents are tied into important, if encapsulated, informal social networks of friends, relatives, and neighbors. Most interact regularly with several neighbors, a few friends, and a few relatives. Perhaps a quarter of each sample could be described as socially isolated. This was true both before and after the move. In the case of the rent subsidy sample and the public housing sample the effect of the move appears to have been to decrease contact somewhat in the first few weeks after the move: thereafter contact increases to approximate or exceed its before-move level. This is particularly clear in the case of neighboring. The data on friendship contact and kin contact are less certain and clear, but they also seem to fit into this dip-rise pattern.

It is not the purpose of this report to go into the theoretical or research problems suggested by these findings. It is sufficient to point out that the informal social life of the subsidy families was not negatively affected by their transfer into middle-income apartment complexes except to a certain extent during the first few weeks of transition. Compared to public housing families, with time spent in the new housing environment, the subsidy families appear to have made relative gains in the areas of neighboring and perhaps friendship interaction. To this extent, the move may have had a beneficial effect on their social lives and involvement.

Voluntary Associations

Other aspects of their social lives might also be examined at this point. What was the effect of the move on memberships in voluntary associations in the area? We have some data on such activity. Each respondent was asked to list the associations to which she belonged and to indicate the extent of her activity. She was given a score based on this report. These scores were computed by giving each respondent one point for each associational membership, two points for attendance at that organization's meetings, three points for contributing, and four points for being an officer. These scores for each organization were summed to get the respondent's total score.

We found that for most of these respondents, before and after the move, civic associations and the like were of relatively little importance. Most reported no contact with local voluntary associations, except for a religious group or church. The before-move scores (excluding church contact) were 2.1 and 2.9 for the subsidy and public housing samples, respectively. The after-move scores were lower, 1.4 and 1.7 respectively. Dividing each sample into subgroups on the length of time elapsed since the move displays an erratic pattern for both groups; however a comparison of the two subgroups who had been moved in for the longest period of time (31 to 61 weeks) suggests a net gain for the subsidy subgroup and a net loss for the public housing group. This may be due to participation by some subsidy tenants in a tenant association group. However the low scores for both groups, before and after the move, indicate that the move probably had little effect on the associational ties of most of these families, either positive or negative.

Contact with Area Institutions

Although the data in the previous section indicate that membership in and attendance at various civic clubs, social clubs, and the like were not very important for most of our subsidy and public housing tenants either before or after their moves, this does not mean that most have had no contacts with social organizations beyond primary social networks. This can be seen in Table 7-1 which lists important organizations and institutions servicing people in the central city of Boston. Because these organizations are locale-bound, we have in this case included the middle-income group as an additional comparison. On the average, members of this better-off group live at approximately the same distance from these organizations as the subsidy respondents.

Looking at the subsidy families, one notes that before the move a majority reported contact only with public institutions, such as the city hospital and the public library. This also was the case with the middle-income and public housing samples. In the case of the other organizations listed in the table, mostly private social service organizations, generally less than a third of any of the black samples reported significant family contacts before the move. It is difficult to assess the meaning of this pattern, without comparable data on low- and middle-income whites, but the overall impression is of rather limited family contact with such social service organizations. It seems evident that in the case of private social service institutions the middle-income and subsidy families had generally had more contacts before the move than had the public housing families.

Caution must be used in assessing the after-move data since the time period involved is usually shorter. In the "before" interview respondents were reporting on the time period that had elapsed since they moved into the "before" apartments. Thus one might well expect in every case a decrease in family contact from the before to after period. In the "after" period families have had

Table 7-1
Contact with Area Institutions

	Subsidy (N=35)	Middle-Income (N=29)	Public (N=24)
Percentage reporting family[a] has had "much to do with" the following places since last move:			
Boston City Hospital	Before 91.4	93.1	91.7
	After 62.9	41.4	54.2
Boston Public Library	Before 68.6	82.8	70.8
	After 68.6	72.4	54.2
St. Mark's Social Center	Before 40.0	34.5	20.8
	After 51.4	48.3	8.3
Charles St. Church	Before 11.4	34.5	4.2
	After 17.1	27.6	8.3
Norfolk House	Before 34.3	34.5	8.3
	After 28.6	27.6	12.5
Blue Hill Protestant Center	Before 0.0	10.3	8.3
	After 2.9	17.2	8.3
Freedom House	Before 48.6	34.5	29.2
	After 34.3	37.9	29.2
Roxbury Boy's Club	Before 31.4	27.6	12.5
	After 25.7	20.7	29.2

[a]Note: One or more persons in family have had contact.

less time to "have much to do" with the organizations listed. This expectation is generally borne out for the two major public institutions, the library and the hospital, for all three housing groups. The pattern for the private organizations is erratic, in some cases the proportion reporting contact going up and in others the proportion going down. Two points about this erratic pattern seem notable. First, in spite of the different time periods involved, a greater proportion of the subsidy families had had contacts with the Charles St. Church and St. Mark's Social Center after the move than before. These organizations had, of course, helped sponsor the Section 221 (d) (3) projects. Second, the pattern of more extensive involvement in service associations for the Section 221 (d) (3) families—both middle income and subsidy—than for the public housing families persists even after the move.

Contrasts among Housing Areas

We can put the detailed comparisons of the subsidy and public groups into perspective by presenting some quick, simplified tabulations for all five groups. Let us return to the contact scores calculated for frequency of interaction with neighbors, relatives, and friends. Here are before/after contact scores for our five categories:

Mean Neighboring Score

	Nonmover	Private	Public	Subsidy	Middle Income
Before	6.9	6.9	7.3	7.0	7.6
After	6.5	5.4	6.1	6.9	7.6

Mean Contact with Kin

	Nonmover	Private	Public	Subsidy	Middle Income
Before	7.6	9.4	12.2	10.3	14.7
After	10.2	11.0	9.7	9.7	14.8

Mean Contact with Friends

	Nonmover	Private	Public	Subsidy	Middle Income
Before	7.1	9.6	12.1	8.1	12.0
After	11.2	11.7	13.0	11.9	17.0

We have already compared the public and subsidy groups. Now we can see that the temporary drop in contact with neighbors and the not-so-temporary rise in contact with friends are both pretty general, while relations with kinsmen vary more sharply from group to group. It looks as though moving into public housing or, for low-income families, moving into 221 (d) (3) developments meant a reduction in daily visits with kinsmen. All but the middle-income families had commonly lived within a few houses of close relatives. The private movers found new dwellings that were still close to those of their relatives, but the public and subsidy families could not do so. The middle-income families were already used to keeping up their contacts with kinsmen more widely separated from them, and were perfectly prepared to continue.

We suspect that the subsidy families will eventually adopt the patterns of their neighbors, and reestablish frequent contacts with their relatives. In fact, a whole series of fragments—membership in voluntary associations, neighboring, worries about lawns, and so on—suggest that they were already taking on some of the "suburban" involvement in the area characteristic of the middle-income families at the time of our interviews. In the short run, however, they remain somewhat less involved with neighbors, friends, and kinsmen than the middle-income families, and resemble the other low-income families, wherever they live, fairly closely.

One very subjective and intriguing question ties a number of these facts and speculations together. We asked the women, "Do you think of this area where you live as a neighborhood? Why?" And the following percentages said it *was* a neighborhood:

	Nonmover	Private	Public	Subsidy	Middle Income
Before	56	50	58	69	52
After	38	69	63	97	79

Once again, while there were some small differences before the move, they widened greatly afterward. All but one of the subsidy respondents labeled her area a neighborhood, middle-income people tended to agree, there was a smaller change in the same direction among the private movers, the public respondents stayed about the same, and the nonmovers, once again, apparently saw their neighborhoods disintegrating around them. Each person, of course, has his own notion of so nebulous a term as "neighborhood." Yet it seems safe to conclude that the subsidy families felt themselves being drawn into a more extensive local social life than they had experienced before.

Changes in Outlook and Aspirations

In addition to questions about social life and housing experiences, we asked the respondents in each of our samples about their general feelings of potency, optimism, and satisfaction before and after the move. Apparently the move into a better housing environment had little effect on overall sense of potency. Each respondent was asked if she agreed or disagreed with the following statement: "No matter how hard you try, there's not much you can do to make a real change for the better." Before and after the move most respondents in both samples disagreed with this statement; 75 percent of the public housing group, before *and* after the move, disagreed, compared with 69 percent of the subsidy group, before *and* after the move. A majority of both groups did *not* feel impotent before and after their moves; this may well have something to do with the fact that, even when they were interviewed before the move, they were expecting to improve their circumstances.

On three other items also asked before and after the moves, one measuring anxiety and two measuring optimism/pessimism, the subsidy sample showed improvement in the direction of decreased anxiety and a somewhat increased sense of optimism, while the public housing sample showed no decrease in anxiety and an increase in pessimism with the move into an ostensibly improved housing environment. The percentages are as follows:

Anxiety/Pessimism Items		Subsidy (N=35)	Public (N=24)
"Sometimes I feel uneasy and sort of afraid without knowing exactly why." (Percentage agreeing)	Before	77	71
	After	57	71

"It's hardly fair to bring a child into the world the way things are for the future." (Percentage agreeing)	Before	51	25
	After	34	33
"It's better to look on the bright side of things and not to be blue all the time." (Percentage *strongly* agreeing)	Before	60	79
	After	74	71

In response to an anxiety item, "Sometimes I feel uneasy and sort of afraid without knowing exactly why," 71 percent of the public housing group agreed both before and after the move, while 77 percent of the subsidy group agreed before the move and only 57 percent agreed afterward, a decrease for the subsidy group. In response to a pessimism item, "it's hardly fair to bring a child into the world the way things are for the future," one-quarter of the public housing group agreed before the move and one-third afterward. The proportion of subsidized families opting for this pessimistic item went down with the move from 51 percent to 34 percent, a substantial decrease. In regard to a general optimism statement, "It's better to look on the bright side of things and not to be blue all the time," we found that the proportion of public housing housewives *strongly* agreeing went down somewhat with the move, from 79 percent to 71 percent, while the proportion of subsidy housewives *strongly* agreeing went up with the move, from 60 percent before to 74 percent afterward. However, it should be noted that almost all families in both groups "tended to agree" or "strongly agreed" with this statement.

Given the responses to these four items, what can be said about the effect of the move on the outlook of these housewives? The pattern of answers suggests that the rent subsidy respondents as a group became more optimistic and less anxious after their moves into a substantially improved housing and social environment, while the public housing respondents as a group remained as uneasy as, and became somewhat more pessimistic than, they were before the move. In this sense, then, the move into a 221 (d) (3) environment seems to have had a favorable effect on the psychological outlook of the low-income housewives receiving a rent subsidy.

Self-Identification

The subsidy and public housing groups can be compared on one other interesting variable. Included in the before and after interviews were some standard questions asking the respondents to estimate the social class of their present neighbors and also their own social class standing. When asked to estimate the class of most people in their neighborhood, they responded as follows:

		Subsidy (N=35)	Public (N=24)
Percentage saying most people in neighborhood are lower class	Before	17	21
	After	0	8
Percentage saying most people are working class	Before	60	46
	After	57	42
Percentage saying most people are middle class	Before	11	21
	After	23	13

Although the concentration of responses, before and after, for both groups is in the working-class category, the shift in perception of neighbors is in the direction one would expect. None of the subsidy tenants, after moving into 221 (d) (3) housing, viewed her neighborhood as lower class; and a larger proportion after the move estimated that most of the neighbors were middle class. This contrasts somewhat with the public housing group; in that group a greater percentage viewed their neighborhood as middle class before the move than did after it. This was compensated for by an increase in the proportion of vague or "don't know" responses among the public housing tenants after the move, an increase found to a lesser extent among the subsidy tenants.

When asked about personal class placement, the black respondents replied as follows:

		Subsidy (N=35)	Public (N=24)
Percentage saying they are lower class	Before	11	13
	After	3	25
Percentage saying they are working class	Before	60	46
	After	71	50
Percentage saying they are middle class	Before	29	25
	After	17	17

Personal class placement also changed with the move. The proportion of rent subsidy tenants describing themselves as lower class went down somewhat with the move (from 11 percent to 3 percent), while the proportion of public housing tenants so classifying themselves went up somewhat with the move. However in both groups the proportions classifying themselves as middle class went *down* with the move. The net result: with the move, an increase in both groups in the proportion identifying themselves as working class. The overall impression one gets from these data on personal and neighborhood class evaluation is the stability of working-class identification for most respondents in both groups, with a somewhat greater relative tendency for the subsidy tenants than for the public housing tenants to evaluate their new environment as higher in social status than their old.

Conclusion

One question which we asked these low-income samples relates to the difficulty in getting settled. The question asked was, "When you moved into this area, how hard did you find it to get settled?" Before the move 13 percent of the public housing sample answered "very hard" or "hard" to the above question; the percentage was the same after the move. The proportion of the rent subsidy sample answering "hard" or "very hard" went up from 9 percent before to 12 percent after the move, a small increase. At the other extreme the proportion reporting that the settling-in process was "easy" or "very easy" went up from 50 percent to 54 percent for the public housing group and from 63 percent to 71 percent for the subsidy sample. The remaining percentages said "not sure" or "just like any other place." Two things are clear from these data. Few of the respondents in both samples found their most recent settling-in process especially difficult, and nearly three-quarters of the experimental subsidy sample viewed their settling-in period as a relatively easy one.

This finding can be extended to the other variables presented earlier in this chapter. The effect on the subsidy respondents and their families seems generally to have been a beneficial one. At the very least, no major negative effects could be determined. The general impact seems to have been positive.

The subsidy respondents—although some were a bit confused about the program—were generally delighted with the subsidy program ("I would like to see it continued forever"), and most thought the fact that they received a subsidy made little or no difference to their higher-status neighbors. Moreover, these very neighbors, when interviewed, were overwhelmingly in favor of rent subsidies for low-income families; only five of the thirty-two middle-income respondents interviewed were even vaguely aware of the presence of subsidy tenants in the projects.

In respect to the physical housing environment, the overwhelming majority of the subsidy respondents were quite pleased with the new environment, the size, the space, the outside of the buildings, the safety and quietness of the streets. Most liked the new apartments much better than their old ones. And few were dissatisfied with the landlord's handling of problems. However, substantial dissatisfaction was expressed in regard to such things as nearness to churches and stores. On most characteristics assessed, public housing respondents were more likely to express dissatisfaction than the 221 (d) (3) subsidy respondents. In addition, the subsidy respondents apparently extrapolated from their own improved circumstances to the position that urban renewal had benefited them personally, and also to the position that urban renewal had benefited their general area. In these respects, the contrast with the more negative evaluations of urban renewal expressed by public housing respondents was great.

The effect on primary social ties of the move into a subsidized 221 (d) (3) apartments was *not* negative over time. The review of primary social ties revealed that most of these black respondents were tied into important, if encapsulated, primary networks of friends, relatives, and neighbors. Most interacted regularly with several neighbors, several friends, and a few relatives. This was true both before and after the moves. The effect of the moves seems to have been to decrease contact somewhat in the first few weeks after the move. Thereafter contact tends to increase to equal or exceed premove levels. The informal social life of the subsidy families was not negatively affected by their transfer into 221 (d) (3) housing, except to a certain extent during the first few weeks of transition. Compared to the public housing respondents, with time spent in the new housing environment, the subsidy respondents appear to have made relative gains in the areas of neighboring and, perhaps, friendship interaction. To this extent, the move may actually have increased the informal social ties of the subsidy families. However, caution dictates that we need to know more about the long-term effect of this process, that is, over several years.

Membership and activity in formal voluntary associations other than the church was negligible for most respondents in the public housing and subsidy samples, both before and after their moves. However, contact with area social service organizations was more extensive, for both the subsidy and public housing families, before and after their moves. Particularly notable was their frequent contact with the Boston City Hospital and the Boston Public Library.

Examination of a few attitudinal items suggested the following pattern: the rent subsidy group tended to become somewhat more optimistic about life in general and less anxious after their move into substantially improved housing (and social environment), while the public housing group tended to remain as uneasy as, and became somewhat more pessimistic than, before the move. This trend certainly parallels the other data; housing improvement and satisfaction are correlated with attitudinal "improvement" among the subsidy families.

The good experience in the new housing also helped to settle the subsidy families down. Up until this time, the low-income families had done a great deal of moving because of family crises, financial problems, and run-ins with landlords. We asked a number of questions about people's past and present searches for housing. Two of them dealt with the future:

Do you expect to be living here five years from now? If no or don't know: Why is that?

Now I'd like you to just let yourself go and think about how you'd like things to be about a year from now. What is the best housing situation you could hope to be in by then? Could you explain how that would happen? Would you say that the chances of that are good?

To get some sense of attachment to the present residence, we can tabulate the "yes" answer to the first question and the "this place is the best I could hope for" answer to the second for the five general housing groups. Here are the percentages:

	Expect to be Here in Five Years		This Place the Best I Could Hope for	
	Before	After	Before	After
Nonmover	12	6	6	19
Private	0	44	0	44
Public	8	46	8	46
Subsidy	3	71	0	91
Middle Income	14	48	0	72

The data are eloquent. Many of the middle-income women told us they hoped to buy their own houses within five years, but otherwise would be satisfied to stay. Some of the subsidy women were not sure where they would be in five years, but none of them said they wanted to move out. In the other groups, many people felt this was just one more move.

Rent subsidies had broken that pattern of one dreary move after another. The small number of people in the program felt they had come upon something far different, and far better, than before. One of them put it better than we could:

It helps a lot to know that you can live happy and decent like one who can really afford it.

8

How the Program Worked and What Difference It Made

Problems of Management

Our respondents' direct contacts with the experimental subsidy program *made little impact on them.* Their indirect contacts with the Boston program *changed their lives.* The initial selection routine meant a few interviews, a lot of uncertain waiting, and a bit of paper-signing: a cumbersome business, but no more than most of the families had been through before in the course of relocation or application for public housing. From that point on, few of the families had any direct contact at all with the Boston Housing Authority. The "problem" families visited by the authority's social worker, and especially the three families ultimately evicted from Academy Homes for unsatisfactory housekeeping, were the main exceptions. Even if we count our repeated interviews as direct contact with the subsidy program, few of the families spent more than a dozen hours dealing with the program's personnel.

Of course, those hours of contact were only one surface of a much larger effort on the part of the people somehow involved in planning and running the program. On the whole the operation did not go badly, considering how many people in different organizations were dealing with the rent supplement program simply as one incidental part of their jobs. We noticed two sore points: the unwieldiness of the selection procedure and the discretionary power of the 221 (d) (3) project managers.

The Boston Housing Authority, as we saw earlier, organized the recruitment and selection of families for the experimental subsidy program. The Boston Redevelopment Authority and the 221 (d) (3) developers, however, did screening of their own, and both acquired a virtual veto over "undesirable" families. In most cases, the passing of dossiers and information from agency to agency dragged on for weeks. The Boston Housing Authority's own screening (which involved checking out of income, employment, and in some cases previous contact with public agencies) was time-consuming and cumbersome. As a result, the candidates for the subsidy program generally waited several months in uncertainty, only to have to move in on short notice if they were accepted.

The power of the project manager caused notable difficulty only in Academy Homes; there an individual personality, rather than the system as a whole, may have been the root of the problem. The manager there complained to us and to others that a minority of the families in the experimental program kept house badly, had acute personal problems, bothered their neighbors, were known as recipients of rent subsidies and were therefore giving the program a bad name, and were making it likely that other better-behaved tenants would leave in disgust. His proposal to evict three families started a flurry of conferences, investigations, and interventions.

The reports assembled by the various officials involved made it fairly clear that the three families did have serious domestic problems, and did not keep their dwellings very neat, but raised some serious doubts about the extent of complaints from their neighbors. In our own inquiries, we found no evidence then or later that other people had identified the three families as "rent subsidy" families or, for that matter, as any other kind of group. We did, however, receive a report that the manager and his secretary, who was an Academy resident, had identified the recipients of rent subsidies to officers of the local tenants' association. The project manager recognized that the three families had domestic problems, but argued—on the ground that he was "not a social worker"—that housekeeping, payment of rent, and acceptability of behavior to the neighbors should be the standards applied to all families. The social workers involved, on the other hand, generally argued that the families needed help, would improve in time, and should not be evicted.

The manager prevailed. One family was evicted, two more were told their leases would not be renewed. The Boston Housing Authority found the evicted family a place in a public housing project. The other two families were still in their Academy dwellings when our observation of the program ended in 1966. So far as we have been able to reconstruct events since then, the later removal of the manager from his post changed the policy. At the end of September 1968, one of the two families was still at Academy. The other family had broken up (a process which was already well underway while they were in Academy), and the woman we had interviewed was living in a private dwelling in Roxbury. Of the three families originally threatened with eviction, then, one had lost, one had won, and for the third it was unclear.

The conflict between the manager's understandable desire to maintain good housekeeping and to establish uniform standards for all tenants and the sponsor's understandable desire to help the families however possible is by no means unique to the use of rent subsidies in middle-income housing. It appears in the administration of public housing itself. It becomes acute, however, when the troubled families who are sponsored happen to be the poorest or most alien residents of a housing development run as a competitive business. The extension of rent subsidies to a wide variety of housing will deepen this dilemma.

These problems affected only a handful of the families in the program. Our evidence indicates that the families receiving rent support were generally good tenants. They paid their share of the rent regularly and without any particular prodding. Their housekeeping appears to have been adequate. We asked our interviewers to place the housekeeping in each dwelling they visited into one of these categories: (1) neat and clean to extreme; (2) neat and clean, but lived-in look; (3) somewhat disorderly, but probably temporarily so; (4) very disorderly and probably not temporarily so. These are, of course, difficult and subjective distinctions. Our interviewers may have become more tolerant in their judgments as they went on, since in all categories of respondents the proportion of households rated as "disorderly" went down substantially from the first interview to the last. For the black families in our basic sample, the percentages described as "somewhat disorderly" or "very disorderly" (with the number of households actually rated in parenthesis) were:

	Before Move	After Move
Private	50% (16)	44% (16)
Public	55% (20)	21% (24)
Middle Income	52% (27)	7% (29)
Subsidy	41% (34)	17% (35)
Nonmovers	60% (15)	27% (15)
Total	50% (112)	20% (119)

Because even the nonmovers received fewer "disorderly" mentions at the later interview, we cannot attach great importance to the apparent rise in neatness among the families that moved. Yet it is clear that by our interviewers' observations the housekeeping of the subsidy families did not pose any exceptional problems. On the contrary, their homes were neater than the average in the postmove period.

Over the two years after our observation of the program ended, the families we have talked to continued to change and move. By the end of September 1968, according to a report prepared for us by Mrs. Harriet Sherburne of the Boston Housing Authority, thirty-five of the original forty families remained in Academy, Marksdale, or Charlame; three of them were by that time paying the full rent, without subsidies. Of the other five families, two were the evicted and the broken family from Academy already mentioned, one was a family evicted from Marksdale for reasons unknown to us, and two others had apparently left their dwellings voluntarily. The "survival rates" were as follows:

Development	Original Number	Number Remaining September 1968	Percent Remaining
Academy	18	14	78%
Marksdale I	7	7	100
Marksdale II	7	6	86
Charlame	8	8	100
Total	40	35	88%

Not all the dropouts need be counted as failures. The three evicted families most likely should be, but the two others may have done what they told us they wanted to: found single-family houses outside the ghetto. Or they may have left Boston entirely. In any case, the question is not only how many families left these dwellings and this program, but also how that compares with the mobility of other families outside the program. It would be enormously informative to trace all of the families we interviewed up to the present, in order to make over a longer run the sort of comparison this report has offered among subsidy, middle income, public, private, and nonmover families. We recommend that it be done. Our guess (which is supported to some extent by the frequency of moves the families reported to us for the period *before* moving into Charlame, Academy, or Marksdale) is that the 88 percent still in their dwellings three to four years after moving in will turn out to be exceptionally high.

Personal Relations

All the subsidy families found themselves in housing they could not have afforded otherwise, with more prosperous neighbors than they would ordinarily have had. We have seen that the families receiving rent subsidies occupied housing that was objectively superior to what they had lived in before, that was generally better than the dwellings acquired by their counterparts in public housing or the private market, and that they themselves rated highly. We have seen that in general the move to the new housing cut down the informal contacts of the families temporarily, but only temporarily; we have some indications that with time their contacts with their kinsmen and neighbors returned to their previous levels, while contact with friends rose to new heights. Coupled with a significant increase in involvement in service associations and supported by a few other fragments of information, this rise in friendship has led us to speculate that the families in the rent subsidy program began to adopt a "suburbanite" way of life on arrival in Charlame, Marksdale, and Academy.

We are, of course, unable to separate neatly the effects of the new housing as such from the effects of being surrounded by neighbors with better jobs, more education, and higher incomes. But the large differences in experience between the families in the experimental program and those who went to public housing (and thus got larger dwellings in far better condition than those they had occupied before) suggest that the interaction between a new kind of housing and a new kind of neighbor was crucial.

As for the new neighbors themselves, neither our interviews nor our other inquiries turned up any evidence of difficulties resulting from the disparities in income, education, and employment between them and the families in the experimental subsidy program. The only likely exceptions are the three families from Academy Homes that we have discussed. To be sure, some of the disparities were not large: on the average, the households in the rent supplement program had one more member, $1,500 less income per year, and a head with two years less education, than their neighbors. They were mainly blacks in mainly black developments. And they only made up 9 percent of the households in those developments.

This experiment obviously cannot tell us what would happen if the income differences were greater, if the families receiving rent subsidies made up half the population, or if one group or the other included more whites. We suspect that any one of these changes would reduce the interaction between members of the two groups somewhat, but we have no reason to think that they would generate a significant amount of friction. In the case at hand, the large majority of higher-income residents easily absorbed the minority of low-income families into their way of life.

The corollary of these observations is that the low-income families as a group had little impact on Charlame, Marksdale, and Academy. The point holds more generally: the experimental program had a large impact on the people in it, and not much effect on anyone or anything else. With forty families involved, it could hardly be otherwise.

The Housing Market

Certainly this applies to the housing market. The net effect on the market was to remove forty potential customers for run-down ghetto dwellings from the market and to put forty middle-income families, mostly blacks, into the market for somewhat better dwellings outside the ghetto core. (The demand for both public housing and 221 (d) (3) dwellings was so great that the experimental program probably had no appreciable influence on the extremely low vacancy rates in either one). We might expect such a shift to increase slightly the pressure for desegregation and for improvement or elimination of substandard dwellings. In an extremely indirect way, therefore, the program acted to improve the stock of housing available to blacks in the metropolitan area. Directly, it added nothing to the stock.

A rent subsidy program run on a hundred times the scale, say, of the present one could influence the housing market significantly. At that scale, we could reasonably assume that the availability of rent subsidies would encourage builders and renovators to produce more new standard units than otherwise would have come onto the market, rather than deflecting potential customers for the newly available standard units toward the stock already in existence.

Expanding the scale would require a choice to be made between devoting the rent subsidies to new construction, rehabilitation, and other sources of standard units. It is, among other things, a choice between subsidizing the production of standard dwellings directly (and making the newly constructed or rehabilitated units immediately available to families now in dilapidated housing) or doing so indirectly (by subsidizing the movement of families now in dilapidated housing into standard dwellings already in the market at prices beyond their means, and expecting a net movement of families now occupying those standard dwellings into newly available units). The "looser" the housing market, and the better the fit between the dwellings already on the market and the needs of families now in rundown housing, the more attractive the second course will be.

The advantages of tying rent subsidies to moderate-income (such as 221 (d) (3)) developments are these:

1. The arrangement guarantees that the families in the program get sound housing.
2. It acts against the segregation of the poor from the rest of the population.
3. It provides some assurance that the total rent charged is a reasonable one.
4. It is somewhat easier to administer than the negotiation of leases with individual landlords.

A housing agency can accomplish any of these objectives without 221 (d) (3) or a similar program at the cost of a considerable burden of inspection, negotiation, and administration. The obvious disadvantages of concentrating rent subsidies in moderate-income developments are:

1. Relative inflexibility in the supply of units from year to year.
2. Little control over the location of the new dwellings available.
3. Difficulties in providing for "undesirable" families when several organizations have a veto over each potential tenant, and the management retains the power to evict.

The final returns from other kinds of rent subsidy programs elsewhere will make the relative weights of these advantages and disadvantages clearer. In the meantime, the Boston experiment seems to justify the devotion of at least a sizable minority of all rent subsidies available to moderate-income developments and also the direct encouragement of developers to construct more units than they would otherwise put up, in order to accommodate recipients of rent subsidies.

Let us speculate a bit. If a thousand new families occupying substandard housing (by 1960 criteria) entered such a program each year for fifteen years, beginning in the 1970s, while other changes in the city's housing stock went on as they have in the past, the city of Boston might expect to have practically no substandard housing left by the late 1980s. At the costs prevailing in the 1960s, a program on that scale would require something like $100 million over the fifteen-year period. These figures are too crude and supposititious to form the basis of a plan. Nonetheless, they indicate that rent subsidies offer a serious alternative to public housing and to "trickle-down" via the private market.

A program on anything approaching this scale might have a serious impact on the pattern of residential segregation in Boston. Under the pattern prevailing in the late 1960s, it would take a net movement of 20,000 households or so to produce an unsegregated city. If *every* unit of the program just imagined were in predominantly white areas and *every* recipient of a rent subsidy were black, the fifteen-year program alone would accomplish roughly three-quarters of that desegregation. Those are big ifs. If, on the other hand, all the newly available units appeared on sites like those of Marksdale, Charlame, and Academy, the result would be a consolidated (but totally renewed) ghetto. Again, these projections build speculation on speculation. Their point is simply to underline the potential impact of a flexible arrangement like the rent supplement on the city's residential segregation.

Our own preference is for racial integration in the housing market. Our respondents, furthermore, generally expressed a preference for integrated and more nearly suburban areas. We recognize, however, the strength of the case many black militants have made for building up organization, wealth, and power *within* the ghetto—as a means of demanding rights long denied. Because of this dilemma, any expanded program of rent subsidies probably should offer (1) considerable influence over the location of the dwelling units in the program to representatives of the black community; (2) considerable choice among locations within and outside the ghetto to recipients of rent subsidies. Even these two requirements, to be sure, may contradict each other, depending on who represents the black community, and how. In that case, the final plan should be a negotiated compromise between the two of them.

Blacks as a group have the worst housing of any of the city's major categories of people. Yet even in Boston the great majority of households occupying substandard housing are white. For that reason, the design of a large-scale program of rent subsidies would present even stickier practical and political problems than we have stated so far. It is not enough to open the program to all comers equally (although that certainly should be done), since the decision to locate the units in one place or another is bound to affect the program's attractiveness to the members of one racial group or another. The expedient of letting those who qualify for the program locate their own housing is likely to do little toward desegregation or even toward breaking down discrimination in supply and cost of housing available to blacks. We would prefer a plan by which, say, half the units were located in or near the present ghetto and the other half scattered through the rest of the city, with blacks encouraged to take units outside the ghetto and whites encouraged to take units inside. But the question is clearly a political one; the political process should include consultation of the people involved.

Alternatives to Rent Subsidies in Boston

These complicated decisions are made even more complicated by the fact that there are some well-established alternatives to various types of direct rent subsidies among the means available for assuring that low-income families get adequate housing. At least these deserve consideration: (1) income redistribution; (2) subsidized rehabilitation of housing in the private market; (3) direct intervention in the private market through such devices as rent controls and tightened inspection; (4) various forms of traditional public housing. Our evaluation study dealt directly with only some of the alternatives—especially one variety of public housing and one way of entering the private market. Our comparisons of rent subsidies with the other alternatives must therefore rest on more general impressions and experience.

Income redistribution via such devices as negative income tax or family allowance has the attractions of administrative simplicity and free choice for the consumer. As a means of improving the housing of poor families, it has several drawbacks. The additional income may not go into housing. The effect on the market is likely to be slow and indirect. It does not guarantee the addition of standard units to the market. There is no assurance that it will diminish the profits of slumlords or reduce the discriminatory barriers within the housing market. Regardless of the desirability of income redistribution on other grounds (and we think it is desirable on other grounds), it will not meet housing needs very directly or effectively.

Subsidized rehabilitation competes more directly with rent subsidies. It assures the addition of standard units to the market, and provides an opportunity for the authority that administers the subsidy to arrange the rental of the units at a reasonable price to families currently in substandard housing. Nevertheless, even with a substantial federal subsidy (in the form of low-interest, long-term loans or cash grants) it is almost impossible for a private owner to bring standard units onto the market at rentals that families like those involved in the Boston experimental program can afford to pay. If the rents can be set equitably, however, rehabilitation combined with direct rent subsidies appears to be an excellent way to improve the housing stock and at the same time offer decent dwellings to poor families. The shorter the supply of standard housing, the more attractive that combination.

We have less hope for direct intervention in the private market through rent controls, tightened housing inspection, antidiscrimination rules, and the like. Although the experience of Call for Action shows that it is possible to get some action from landlords through well-placed complaints to them and the authorities, code enforcement in Boston and other big cities appears to be at best a holding operation unlikely to produce a significant improvement in the general stock of housing.[1]

The Massachusetts provisions for withholding rent from landlords who maintain their properties poorly do add a powerful sanction to code enforcement, and weaken the threat of eviction for tenants who complain. Again, they are more likely to eliminate one kind of exploitation than they are to influence significantly the general stock of housing or the ability of low-income families to find sound dwellings. The same may be said for rent controls. Open-housing legislation and listing agencies like Fair Housing, Incorporated, serve an important purpose for blacks who can already afford sound housing and wish to leave the ghetto. Except for rent controls, all of these are efforts to purify the market: to make sure that those who have the money get their money's worth. Rent subsidies are different; they give more buying power to those who do not have the money. The two kinds of programs therefore complement each other.

Traditional low-rent public housing, on the other hand, operates mainly to provide sound housing for those who do not have the money. After the long years in which the large, segregated project virtually monopolized public housing efforts, public housing has recently started to come in a variety of packages. Not only have many cities (including Boston) built vestpocket developments, but they have developed programs of buying or leasing, and sometimes rehabilitating, scattered dwellings.

The current leasing program of the Boston Housing Authority, which began in 1966, was originally expected to draw mainly on existing standard vacancies in the private market. At the beginning, few owners of standard private dwellings actually offered their units to the authority. The authority had much greater success in newly-constructed 221 (d) (3) developments. Indeed, the families remaining in the rent subsidy program in 1967, at the end of the three-year demonstration period, were transferred into the leasing program.[2] By 1968 the BHA had 725 occupied leased units, of which about 500 were 221 (d) (3). And by the early 1970s the figure had reached 2000 units. Those totals, and new commitments running into the thousands, make it appear that the leasing program may eventually have a serious impact on Boston's housing market. One slight advantage of the leasing program, at least in theory, is that it reduces the landlord's opportunity to veto a prospective tenant or to evict an existing tenant arbitrarily, yet compensates him for his loss of power by assuring him of rent continuously for the term of the lease, even if the unit is vacant. Since the only significant administrative difficulties which showed up in the course of our observation of the experimental subsidy program had to do with selection and rejection, this advantage deserves attention.

Public construction and management of housing, of course, has the same advantage. Within the limits set by the grants of funds, the Boston Housing Authority has complete control over the selection and retention of tenants. That is a good thing when the selection process is efficient and equitable, and when it does not exclude "problem" families; unfortunately, the Boston Housing Authority has fallen down on all three points at times. Public housing of the classic variety also guarantees that the housing made available to the poor is sound. But big-project public housing has some notorious disadvantages: unattractive design, segregation of the poor, stigmatization of the tenants, forced departure when income passes a certain level.

The purchase or construction of scattered units can overcome most of these difficulties, especially if the tenant gets an option to buy his dwelling at a fair market price. Scattered-site public housing also has some obvious costs: extensive, continuous involvement of the Housing Authority in small real-estate transactions, expensive management and maintenance, great difficulty in giving tenants what they prefer and yet treating all applicants for public housing equitably. It is much easier to have a few large projects in which all units are about equally desirable, or equally undesirable.

Our Families' Preferences

Our own inquiry showed that the families placed in large public housing developments generally considered their new dwellings better than their old ones and found the rents attractive. They had about the same amount of space as before, and paid about the same rents, but all of them had moved into dwellings in better physical condition than those they occupied before. Nevertheless, our public housing families were the least enthusiastic about their new homes of our four groups of movers—public housing, private market, middle income. Their tepid approval of the new dwelling and its surroundings contrasted sharply with the general pleasure of the comparable families receiving rent subsidies.

The reports given to us by our respondents concerning their own immediate situations jibed fairly well with their more general expressions of preference for one kind of housing or another. On each of the interviews, for example, we asked a question about housing preferences.

For the sample as a whole, the least popular alternatives were an apartment outside of Roxbury and a public housing development. The most popular choices were a new housing development like Marksdale or a house in the suburbs. These priorities held both before and after the move. Given a free choice, these families would rather have a house than an apartment, and would rather be in the suburbs than in the city. But if it is to be in the city, they find new row-house construction à la Marksdale very attractive.

To some extent, the families' preferences matched their current experience. The nonmovers, who were mainly in houses and apartments in Roxbury and its immediate vicinity, retained a greater preference for that same kind of housing than did members of the other categories. Families destined for public housing started out no more favorable to it than the average, but simply by remaining the same after the move they ended up considerably more favorable to public housing than anyone else. The most striking cases are the two groups (middle income and subsidy) actually moving into 221 (d) (3) housing, who were already overwhelmingly favorable to "developments like Marksdale" before the move and remained so afterward.

Moving from apartments to row houses (which was the change the great majority made) seems to have made these same families less interested in apartment living. Once they had moved into the 221 (d) (3) developments, the

Table 8-1

Percentage Saying They Would Like to Live in Various Types of Housing and Dwelling Areas, Before and After Moving (120 Black Families Only)

Housing and Area	When Asked	Private (N=16)	Public (N=24)	Middle Income (N=29)	Subsidy (N=35)	Nonmover (N-16)	Total (N=120)
Apartment in	Before	50	38	34	51	62	46
Roxbury	After	38	33	28	29	50	33
Apartment Somewhere	Before	31	46	28	46	56	41
Else in the City	After	31	54	17	23	31	30
A Public Housing	Before	38	42	21	51	50	40
Development	After	12	42	7	14	25	19
An Apartment in	Before	38	58	69	57	81	61
the Suburbs	After	44	50	31	29	50	38
One of the New Housing Developments like Marksdale	Before	44	67	86	84	81	75
	After	50	58	86	91	69	75
A House in	Before	50	42	55	46	75	52
Roxbury	After	44	38	45	57	75	51
A House Somewhere	Before	50	64	45	46	50	50
Else in the City	After	50	42	48	49	81	52
A House in the	Before	75	67	79	66	75	72
Suburbs	After	75	75	83	71	69	75
In the	Before	56	38	45	54	31	46
Country	After	56	71	45	51	56	55

members of both the subsidy and middle-income groups said much less often than they had before the move that they would like to live in each of the apartment choices—in Roxbury, elsewhere in the city, in the suburbs and, especially, in public housing. All groups grew somewhat less interested in apartments with the move, but the families going to 221 (d) (3) made the strongest and most consistent shift in that direction.

The *dislikes* are also illuminating. For two of the main alternatives we are considering, here are the proportions saying they would *not* like to live in that sort of housing:

Housing and Area	When Asked	Private	Public	Middle Income	Subsidy	Nonmovers	Total
Public Housing	Before	56	25	52	37	25	39
	After	88	42	83	77	69	72
Housing developments like Marksdale	Before	50	17	10	17	12	19
	After	38	33	10	3	25	18

To all groups, even including the families who actually moved into public housing, the choice of public housing came to seem less desirable once they had moved. Neither before nor after the move did many families reject developments like Marksdale. However we look at it, we find the sort of 221 (d) (3) dwellings that went up in Roxbury an extremely popular choice, an alternative greatly preferred to public housing, indeed to almost any kind of dwelling except a house in the suburbs.

Relative Costs

What about expense? We have no usable information on the cost of providing standard housing through income redistribution or direct intervention in the private market. We have some data on the apparent costs of large project public housing, leased housing, and experimental rent subsidies in Boston. The data have two important flaws: (1) they deal with current costs for units already on hand, rather than the cost of adding new units by each method; (2) they do not genuinely reflect the differences in administrative costs among the programs. In costs per unit per month, the figures are:

Housing Program	Administrative Costs	Level of Subsidy	Total
Public Housing			
Nonelderly units built 1940-54	$7.40	$24.87	$32.27
Elderly units built 1960-63	7.40	62.12	69.52
Elderly units built 1965	7.40	69.78	77.18
Elderly units built 1966	7.40	75.52	82.92
Total public housing	7.40	26.91	34.31
Leased Housing			
First 9 private units leased, first 3 months	7.37	50.56	57.93
First 5 221 (d) (3) units leased first month	7.37	60.20	67.57
Estimated cost of first thousand units	7.37	54.00	61.37
Rent subsidies in 221 (d) (3)	7.37	51.01	58.38

Note: Calculated from figures provided us by Mr. Frank Donahue, Director of Finance and Accounts, Boston Housing Authority.

No one should lean on these figures very heavily for fear that they might collapse. The low subsidy of the nonelderly public housing units comes largely from the fact that they were built some time ago, when construction costs were lower than today. As the table shows, the support rises regularly with the recency of construction; the apparent costs of recently constructed housing for the elderly greatly surpass those of leasing and rent subsidies.

Again, we have no reason to expect any substantial difference in support between the rent subsidy and leasing programs for 221 (d) (3), although the table shows an apparent difference of almost $10 per month. We have good reason, on the other hand, to expect the administration of leasing scattered private units to cost more than the administration of leasing units in 221 (d) (3); the table goes the other way. The main value of the figures, therefore, is to show that the costs of all the alternatives under consideration fall into the same general range.

Conclusion

Given the current housing situation of American central cities, and particularly the housing problems of blacks in those cities, direct rent subsidization looks like a good tool for some time to come. The Boston experiment worked remarkably smoothly from the viewpoint of almost everyone involved. None of the dangers that people had imagined rent subsidies might bring (for example, demoralization of the families, or friction with richer neighbors) materialized. The Boston experiment had no impact on the city's pattern of residential segregation, but an enlarged program of the same kind could make a great difference in that regard. In cities like Boston, we think it would be reasonable to devote at least half the money that becomes available toward enlarging the supply of publicly subsidized housing to rent supplementation, leasing, or equivalent programs, and to let the choice between new housing and housing already available depend on the tightness of the market and the availability of sponsors.

9

Low-Income Housing Programs: Review and Conclusions

Before 1966 poor families displaced by public action faced a hard choice between unsubsidized housing in the private market and subsidized housing under public ownership and management. Those choosing private housing were forced to accept substandard housing elsewhere or pay significantly more for the relocation housing, or both. Those choosing traditional public housing typically received units in large, institutional developments which segregated so-called problem families from the rest of society. The general impact of these forced choices—spreading slum areas on the one hand, or storing poor people out of sight on the other—has been well documented. Other poor families not threatened by urban renewal or other public action have been confronted by the same unhappy choices, for the poor continue to dwell in housing that is substandard, overpriced, or segregated.[1]

Since the mid-1960s several new housing programs designed for "low-income" or "lower-income" families have been authorized by Congress, each involving income redistribution in the form of federal payments on behalf of housing. However, several of the "low-income" programs, such as the 221 (d) (3) BMIR Program (taken alone), the Section 235 Homeownership Program, and the Section 236 Rental Housing Program have not in practice been viable alternatives for most poor families who face the problematical choices noted above. They are not real alternatives to traditional low-rent public housing because the limited federal subsidization involved means that housing generally cannot be rented or sold for sums that most families in the public housing income range can be expected to pay. These new programs are in fact moderate-income programs.

In our view, thus, only two of the current major "low-income" programs provide workable alternatives to traditional public housing or substandard private housing—the Rent Supplement Program and the Section 23 Leasing Program. The Rent Supplement Program was created by the 1965 Housing Act and is administered directly through federal agencies, generally bypassing local public housing authorities. The program relies on private groups and organizations to build and manage low-rent housing units. Contracts for rent subsidy payments are made directly between a federal agency and private owners. Unlike the Rent Supplement Program, the Section 23 Leasing Program is administered through the same local housing authorities that handle conventional public housing. This approach provides for leasing by the local authorities of existing housing units from private owners, followed by the subleasing of these units to poor tenants who would otherwise qualify for public housing.

139

Even before these new low-income housing programs began operation in the 1966-67 period, the experimental rent subsidy program in Boston anticipated many of their most important features and characteristics.

The Boston Experimental Program

Until 1964 the Boston Housing Authority had put most of its energy into large public housing developments. Then it began an experiment with rent subsidies, financed by the federal Department of Housing and Urban Development (then called the Housing and Home Finance Agency) with funds allocated by Congress in the early 1960s for experimental housing programs. For the three-year period 1964-67, forty large, low-income families displaced by public action (thirty-five of them black, five mixed or white) paid the rents they would normally have paid in public housing, but lived in apartments or row houses in one of three newly constructed 221 (d) (3) middle-income developments. The three projects were sponsored by nonprofit organizations with a definite interest in Boston's black community and were located in the ghetto or on its fringe. Two of them were, in fact, side by side in the midst of a cleared site within a major ghetto urban renewal project.

The Boston Housing Authority undertook its experiment in a city in which the housing stock was slowly improving. Still, blacks not only occupied the worst dwellings but were getting the least out of improvements that were occurring. The ghetto, which occupied adjacent rundown sections of the South End, Roxbury, and Dorchester, had consolidated in the 1950s and showed no signs of fragmentation in the 1960s. In 1964, when the rent subsidy program began, about 3,000 of the city's roughly 65,000 blacks lived in public housing. Virtually no new public housing for general occupancy had been built for a decade, and only a few of the existing public housing units were close to the ghetto. Half of the city's black families have had no practical alternative to deteriorating housing at excessive rents.

Furthermore, the urban renewal programs of the 1960s were concentrating on the principal areas where blacks lived. The short-run effect was to remove bad housing the black poor could barely afford and to replace it with a smaller amount of good housing they could not afford. The Washington Park renewal program, in the center of the ghetto, destroyed over 2,000 of the city's worst dwellings from 1960 to 1966 and put up about 800 dwellings for families with incomes of $5,000 or more per year. Few of the 2,000 displaced families were in that income range; the net effect of the razing and relocation was to expand the ghetto into adjacent areas of substandard housing. Private programs like that of Call for Action or Fair Housing Incorporated (no longer in existence) and the Boston Redevelopment Authority's relocation service were working in the right direction but had little impact on the pattern of segregation, discrimination, and inequality in the Boston housing market.

The Boston Housing Authority's rent subsidy program did not have much impact on segregation, discrimination, and inequality, either. But the experiment did provide important signs that direct rent subsidies on a much larger scale could well make a significant difference in all three regards and that the families themselves would generally prefer the arrangement to other means of getting standard housing.

The Boston rent subsidy program dealt with a common situation in what may become a typical way. Although its designers did not realize how typical it would become when they were planning in 1963, certain critical features of their resulting program were prophetic: (1) provision of housing for families displaced by public action; (2) restriction to families with incomes low enough for admission to public housing; (3) payment of federally-financed rent subsidies directly to development owners on behalf of selected tenants; and (4) substantial local housing authority control over tenant selection, rent, and administrative procedures.

Subsequently, both the Rent Supplement Program and the Section 23 Leasing Program incorporated some of these extraordinarily important features. Both were designed for poor families with incomes in the public housing range; both have facilitated housing poor families displaced by public action. The Rent Supplement Program formally focuses on such families. Both programs involve federal rent support for low-income families. Under the Rent Supplement Program, subsidies are typically paid to the development owners, while under the Section 23 Leasing Program support comes through the leasing arrangements of the local housing authority. In regard to the fourth characteristic, local housing authority control, the Boston experimental program was similar to the Section 23 Leasing Program and differed from the final version of the Rent Supplement Program.

The experimental Boston program was different from the Rent Supplement and Section 23 Leasing Programs in other respects. The Boston program, unlike the Rent Supplement Program as it was operating in the late 1960s, was not as severely hemmed in by federal restrictions on construction costs, maximum market rentals, and housing amenities—limitations that may not only have virtually eliminated the possibility of building qualifying housing that will attract the income mix of the Boston experimental program but also have made the Rent Supplement Program unworkable for new construction in most central cities outside the South. The Boston program reflected greater flexibility in this regard, a flexibility to which the Rent Supplement Program will probably have to return if it is to serve a large number of low-income families. The Boston experiment also contrasted with many leasing programs in its involvement entirely with new construction and its contractual arrangements (the private owners, or their managers, played an important role in selecting tenants and in the administration of the Boston project).

The Boston program was also prophetic in that two circumstances associated with its implementation seem characteristic of many local projects built under subsequent low-income housing programs: (1) a very high proportion of black families as participants, and (2) housing built on a renewal site, frequently in or near a ghetto area.

The three ghetto housing developments involved in the experimental program, newly constructed 221 (d) (3) middle-income housing, varied in design (Charlame Park Homes and Marksdale Gardens were mainly row houses while Academy Homes consisted of two-and three-story apartments), but all three were attractive and convenient. Largely because of their locations, they attracted mostly black tenants—close to 90 percent.

The forty families were scattered through the three developments, occupying about one unit in eleven. Aside from a few administrative accidents, the only segregation was due to the families' need for larger apartments, which were clustered to some extent; but our research indicated that there were no areas that could reasonably be labeled "rent subsidy areas." So far as we could determine, no areas ever were labeled that way by local residents. Nor were the recipients of rent subsidies ever singled out by their neighbors as a separate class of people.

The normal rents in Charlame, Marksdale, and Academy ran from $85 to $150 per month. For the forty families, the Boston Housing Authority paid (using federal money) the difference between those rents and the amounts the families would normally pay in conventional public housing. The rent subsidy averaged about $51 per month per family.

The experimental rent subsidy program lasted three years. Because of the construction schedule, the last families moved in when it had little more than a year to run. At the end of the three-year period, thirty-five families of the original forty still remained in the program. Three had, in effect, been evicted for bad housekeeping; two more had, so far as we can tell, dropped out voluntarily. When the program officially ended, the Boston Housing Authority shifted the remaining families to a new leasing arrangement so that none of them had to move from the dwellings they were currently occupying. By September 1968, three of the thirty-five families had sufficient income to pay the full rent themselves; altogether, then, 88 percent of the families who started the program in 1964 and 1965 were still in their dwellings three or four years later.

The Evaluation Study

Our systematic observation of the rent subsidy program ran from the summer of 1964 (two months before the first families moved into their new dwellings) to the summer of 1966 (eight months after the last families moved in). During that time, we stayed in contact with the people running the program, examined records of the Boston Housing Authority and of several other agencies dealing with the housing of low-income families in Boston, collected general information about the Boston housing market, and interviewed a number of officials and local leaders concerned with housing and other problems of Boston's ghetto. Our largest effort, however, went into a series of interviews with forty families in the rent subsidy program and with other families chosen for comparison.

In addition to the forty basic families, we sought out similar families moving into public housing, others finding dwellings in the private market, still others not moving, and a group of higher-income families moving into the same three new developments as the families receiving rent subsidies. The various waves of interviewing were staged before the move, shortly after the move, and at a period of six months or so after the move. We also did some follow-up interviewing at the very end of our observation period. Most of our analysis in this report dealt with the 129 families that were best matched with respect to income, color, size, and composition and with whom we had comparable interviews both before and after the move; a number of the comparisons, however, treated only with the 120 black families in that category. For the purposes of this report, we have concentrated on two sorts of comparison: (1) between the same families before and after the move into different kinds of housing, and (2) among the five major housing categories—subsidy, middle income, private market, public housing, and nonmovers. Our detailed information stops in the summer of 1966. Our analysis therefore deals with the relatively short-run impact of this type of rent subsidy program; we cannot be sure what its effect over a span of five or ten years will be.

Findings

In general, our investigation showed that the experimental rent subsidy program met its objectives of providing sound, attractive housing to poor families without major difficulties and at moderate cost. The selection process was relatively cumbersome, partly as a result of being grafted onto the Boston Housing Authority's regular procedures for placing families in public housing. But once families had joined the program, there was little that could go wrong. The chief mishap was the attempted eviction of a few families for "bad housekeeping." That case points, perhaps, to the desirability of putting more control over the conditions of tenure in the hands of government housing authorities. In general, the poor families in the program kept their dwellings in good condition. They paid their rents regularly, and from every point of view fulfilled their obligations as tenants. In short, the administration of the program did not present any exceptional problems, and it required much less apparatus than does the running of conventional public housing developments.

The average rent subsidy of just over $50 per month, plus estimated administrative expenses, brought the cost of the program to something like $58 per unit per month. Direct subsidies of this sort appear to be a less expensive way of adding dwellings to the stock available to poor families than is construction of new publicly owned developments. At least they appear to have the advantage over the short run of five to ten years. In the long run, obviously, capital costs per unit of publicly owned housing decline, even if maintenance costs rise, while rent subsidies tend to remain constant, or rise with average rents; the financial advantage of one or the other will depend on borrowing cost, the durability of the publicly owned housing, and the rate of increase in rents.

Public construction of new housing, however, does guarantee the addition of new, sound units to the housing stock for low-income families. Rent subsidies in themselves do not. The Boston experiment essentially opened up to low-income families forty units that probably would have been built anyway, would have had the same locations, and would have been occupied by families with incomes well above the poverty line. Its indirect effect on the housing market was therefore probably to displace forty middle-income families, mostly blacks, into the metropolitan market for sound privately owned dwellings. However, a rent subsidy program on a much larger scale directed toward new dwellings could encourage construction for low-income families that would otherwise not occur.

Almost all the families in the various housing groups we studied came from the ghetto or its fringe. The net effect of all their moves was to displace the group somewhat away from the central ghetto into the adjacent sections of the city. On the average, the sample of families moving into public housing actually went farthest from the ghetto, because there are relatively few public housing units in Boston's areas of greatest black concentration. Because of the locations of the three middle-income developments, the subsidy families all stayed in or near the ghetto. People in all housing groups tended to report more contact with whites after the move; again, there was nothing special about the rent subsidy families in this respect. The truth is that *not one* of the alternatives under consideration produced a significant amount of residential desegregation.

They did, however, produce important changes in the quality of the housing people occupied, and in how much they like it. Most families in every housing category moved into better housing than they had before—better in terms of structural soundness, space, comfort, and the family's satisfaction with it. The people who really got a bad deal—and knew it—were those who had expected the Boston Housing Authority or the Boston Redevelopment Authority to find them new dwellings but had not been placed. The rent subsidy families, on the average, experienced far larger improvements than anyone else—except in terms of rent paid and convenience of location. On the whole, the families who went to public housing were least satisfied, except that they found their rents satisfactory and their locations convenient. The subsidy families had some minor complaints about the design of their new dwellings, but their general attitude was quite enthusiastic.

Most people cut some informal social ties at the move, and slowly made new friends afterward. Those who moved through the private market—and thus had the greatest control over their new locations and relied very often on friends and relatives in the search for housing—appear to have cut the fewest ties. Those who moved into public housing appear to have cut the most. In the new neighborhood, our data indicate that the subsidy families joined in local affairs faster and more actively than poor families moving into some other types of housing, and that the net effect of the move was a heavier involvement in friendship activities than they had carried on before. We could detect no signs that the higher-income neighbors of the subsidy families singled them out as a special group, or that any special frictions developed from the neighboring of households with different income levels. Of course, the income differences were modest, and the so-called middle-income families had seen enough of the housing problems of poor blacks to be quite favorable to the general principle of direct rent subsidization.

Policy Implications

The Boston Housing Authority's experiment with direct rent subsidies let a small shaft of light into a very dark corner. For almost all of the families involved, it provided housing far better than they had before, housing they liked very much, at a cost not much different from that of providing new units of public housing. If the experimental program provided a fair test, this particular device for making standard housing available to poor families deserves use on a much larger scale. So far we have concentrated on whether direct rent subsidies work, without too much bother and expense, as a means of providing sound housing for poor families. In our view, they certainly do. We should also consider their implications for other persistent problems of housing policy: relocation, desegregation, economic integration, code enforcement, and special-need households.

The subsidy families in the Boston experiment, and many of those in other housing markets with whom we compared them, were being relocated as a consequence of urban renewal in and around the ghetto. Our findings indicate that the families who relocated through the private market had the smallest personal adjustment to make, because they were continuing a routine they already knew well from previous moves. The low-income families moving into public housing and middle-income apartment complexes had greater adjustments to make. In almost every respect the families moving into 221 (d) (3) dwellings were far happier with those adjustments. The really unhappy group was composed of the families who had expected to be relocated, but had not moved at all. While relocation has its costs, once the move out has begun, nonrelocation is costlier still.

Several features of rent subsidies make them handy tools for the relocation of poor families. They are flexible: in all but a very tight market they can rapidly increase the number of units available for relocated families. They give the redevelopment and housing authorities the means of assuring that the relocated families receive dwellings in good condition. The location of the dwellings, furthermore, is not a great problem. In principle, it makes little difference whether they are scattered or clustered, central or suburban. The main limit in all these respects is the state of the city housing market.

Whether rent subsidy programs produce racial desegregation in housing depends entirely on the location of the subsidized units. The Boston experimental program did not produce any substantial amount of desegregation. Programs working with the existing stock of housing, even if run by people committed to equal opportunity, are likely to feel the subtle pressures that produce current forms of residential segregation—if only because their policy itself will affect units which are offered for leasing or subsidy. A greatly expanded and well-designed program of rent subsidization could have a strong impact on the pattern of racial segregation. The more scattered the units, the greater the desegregation, so long as a substantial proportion of the families involved belonged to racial minorities. A policy of clustering, on the other hand, would tend to perpetuate—or even consolidate—the ghetto.

The Boston experiment did produce a small but promising measure of economic integration: families of somewhat different income levels living together without notable difficulty in the new 221 (d) (3) middle-income developments. *We have no reason to believe that it could not happen on a larger scale.* This feature of rent subsidization deserves further scrutiny, because the Boston arrangements were especially favorable: a modest income gap between poor and nonpoor families, a low proportion of poor families, no notable racial difference between the two groups. We suspect that changing any one of these conditions significantly would reduce the contact between the families receiving rent subsidies and their neighbors. Some public assumptions notwithstanding, however, we also suspect that it would take a huge change in these conditions to produce systematic hostility between the two groups. The best way to find out is to examine carefully the cases in other cities in which the proportions have been different, the income differentials larger, the racial cleavage more definite.

It is also hard to judge the effect of an expanded program of rent subsidization on the quality of a city's housing. For the particular dwellings involved in programs like the Boston experiment, the local housing authority control over rent payments and tenure gives the city a new means of assuring that landlords in the private market respect the building and health codes. Such a program ought to reduce the demand of very poor families for substandard dwellings, but whether landlords would typically respond to rising vacancy rates by improving, converting, abandoning, razing, or by reducing the rents on their properties is difficult to say. No doubt a combination of all of these would occur, and the net effect might be a modest improvement in housing quality.

This brings up a danger many people have seen in direct rent subsidies. What if they gave unscrupulous landlords an opportunity to collude with inspectors in setting high rents and low standards? The association of subsidies with housing built by nonprofit or limited-dividend corporations does not pose much of a threat. But what about slum properties operated for maximum profit? There is a risk here, and it necessitates policing. A local housing authority operating a rent subsidy program under its own control has several advantages over the city's code enforcement officer. It is offering something precious to a slum landlord: a guarantee of continuous rent payments. It can negotiate the rent directly—with plenty of experience lying behind the negotiations—for many units at a time, rather than relying on piecemeal landlord-tenant agreements. It can supervise maintenance of the housing units itself, or contract with a third party for maintenance.

Actually, fluctuations in the eagerness of landlords to offer their properties are probably a greater risk than corruption and collusion. The experience of one of North America's largest and oldest experiments with rent subsidies, in Toronto, Canada, was that plenty of rent properties were available when the housing market was depressed, but that when it became more active landlords began to withdraw their properties, or to push up their rents, at the expiration of their leases. For that reason, an authority relying heavily on the private market would be well advised to negotiate long-term leases with widely varying expiration dates.

Households with special needs may not be so well served by the rent subsidy approach. Old people are perhaps the best example. Low-rent public housing built specifically for the elderly often has such features as ramps, few and easy stairways, low cabinets, specially equipped bathrooms. Although there are excellent reasons for avoiding the construction of large enclaves of old people, there are also many advantages—social, practical, financial—to producing such dwellings in small clusters. Rent subsidies of the type in the Boston experiment do not lend themselves to this purpose very easily. They work best at providing for households who need the sorts of dwellings which normally come onto the market but which, without subsidy, would be beyond the means of low-income families.

Current Progress in Low-Income Housing

By way of conclusion it might be well to review briefly the current status of low-income housing programs in the United States, particularly the two established programs which are similar to the Boston experiment and which we view as workable alternatives to the traditional public housing approach. In this book's introductory chapter we reviewed the recent history of low-income housing programs and pointed out that it is only in the last six or seven years that there have been major shifts in American housing programs.

Since their inception, how successful have the various housing programs been in reducing America's housing poverty? How much progress is currently being made in meeting housing needs? How much money has the federal government expended? How many housing units have been constructed under these programs? These questions are not as easy to answer from federal statistics as one might expect. The question of money expended is perhaps the easiest to answer.[2] Table 9-1 details annual federal expenditures or obligations for the five major housing subsidization programs, divided into two basic categories,—those which basically aid low-income families and those which support families with incomes somewhat above the conventional poverty line (sometimes called "low-income" or "lower-income" programs in the literature). It is evident from these data that the older low-rent public housing (LRPH) program still receives the lion's share of federal housing expenditures on behalf of low- and moderate-income families. In fiscal 1971 federal obligations in the LRPH program exceeded half a billion dollars. The new Section 23 Leasing Program, also controlled by local housing authorities, received substantially less federal fiscal support—just over 100 million dollars. As can be seen, since 1969 the leasing program has rapidly expanded. The other truly low-income program, that providing for rent supplements, rated a poor third among the three low-income programs in fiscal 1971, accounting for only 7 percent of total federal housing dollars in this area.

As we have noted previously, relatively few families in the Section 235 Homeownership and Section 236 Rental Housing Programs have incomes near the median incomes of families in the three truly low-income programs. However, even in the first three years of operation these moderate-income (loan interest reduction) programs have seen dramatic increases in federal expenditures. Indeed, in fiscal 1971 more was spent by the federal government on supporting the new Section 235 Homeownership Program than for either of the new low-income programs.

How many low- and moderate-income *families* have actually been aided by these divergent housing approaches? With one or two exceptions, it is difficult to determine the actual number of units completed under these federal housing programs—figures which can (assuming a low-vacancy rate) be used as a proxy for the number of families receiving aid. The figures on all public housing programs (traditional and leasing) indicate that the number of units actually under management more than doubled between the calendar years 1960 and 1971:

1971	992,700
1970	896,300
1965	604,900
1960	478,200

Less than 10 percent of these units under public management (75,900 in 1970) has been supplied under the new Section 23 Leasing Program. In 1971, thus,

Table 9-1
Annual Federal Expenditures in Assisted HUD Programs, 1963-1971 (in thousands of dollars)

Fiscal Year	Low-Rent Public Housing (LRPH)	Low Income Programs		Moderate Income Programs	
		Leased Public Housing (Sect. 23)	Rent Supplement	Rental Housing (Sect. 236)	Homeownership (Sect. 235)
1971	$523,338	$103,013	$42,289	$13,576	$119,818
1970	393,396	79,495	18,609	679	21,909
1969	324,476	55,140	4,804		812
1968	280,172	21,991	1,037		
1967	254,345	6,481	120		
1966	231,594	407			
1965	217,916				
1964	190,896				
1963	176,482				

Source: Division of Research and Statistics, Federal Housing Administration, Department of Housing and Urban Development. The figures for the public housing programs represent annual net obligations, while the figures for the other programs represent actual (annual) federal expenditures.

nearly a million poor families, half white and half nonwhite, were being served by these public housing programs.

The much smaller number of poor families being aided by means of rent supplements can be seen in the following figures we obtained from HUD's Division of Research and Statistics, figures on the number of housing units actually under payment. Data on two moderate-income federal programs have been included for comparison:[3]

	Rent Supplement Program	Section 236 Rental Housing Program	Section 235 Homeownership Program
June 1967	929	−0−	−0−
June 1968	2,731	−0−	−0−
June 1969	12,299	−0−	5,454
June 1970	30,459	5,437	65,654
June 1971	52,740	32,322[a]	204,832

[a]About 5,000 families in Section 236 rental units also received rent supplements. They are not included in this figure.

Even in the most recent fiscal year only 50,000 low-income families were being aided under the Rent Supplements Program, compared to nearly one million low-income families in public housing and more than 230,000 moderate-income families in the Section 235 and Section 236 Programs. Percentage growth in these latter two moderate-income programs has been truly incredible. Between June 1970 and June 1971 the number of units under payment for rent supplements increased by 72 percent, while the number in the Section 236 Program increased 494 percent and the number in the Section 235 Homeownership Program increased by 212 percent. Even in all the low-income and moderate-income programs taken together, no more than 1.3 million families were receiving federal assistance.

The data we have been able to secure, therefore, lend support for the conclusions about and assessments of low-income and moderate-income programs in the recent housing report of the President's Committee on Urban Housing, aptly entitled *A Decent Home*:

A slippage in program direction and Congressional funding, up and away from serving families in the most dire need of assistance.

A woefully inadequate scale of all Government housing subsidy programs.[4]

These conclusions become particularly poignant when one realizes that even the relatively limited LRPH and Rent Supplement Programs, those with the deepest-reaching subsidies, provide little assistance for the *poorest of the poor* families—those with incomes below $1500 a year.

Conclusion

The basic conclusion we reached in our assessment of Boston's rent subsidy experiment was that this device for making sound housing available to poor families worked well and has every possibility of working well on a larger scale. It deserves use on a much larger scale. Both the current Rent Supplement Program and the Section 23 Leasing Program share certain basic features of Boston's experimental programs, perhaps the most important of which is the utilization of sound housing in the private market. Yet the HUD figures show that neither one of these programs is coming anywhere near providing the amount of new dwelling units needed. With the number of Americans in poverty still between 20 and 30 million (depending on which poverty line is used) and the number of families in substandard, deteriorating, overcrowded, or overpriced housing at least 7 to 8 million, much additional private and public effort is needed, if American's housing poverty is to be met. Indeed, the 1968 report of the Committee on Urban Housing stressed the specific goals which must be pursued:

We recommend that the nation commit itself to a goal of producing at least 26 million new and rehabilitated housing units by 1978, including six to eight million Federally subsized dwellings for families in need of housing assistance.[5]

On an annual basis this would mean an increase in annual production rates from then current 100,000 to 150.000 subsidized units for low- and moderate-income families to at least 600,000 to 800,000 units—a jump of several hundred percent. The cost of such programs by 1978—the report estimated—would be in the neighborhood of 3 to 5 billion dollars.

One way to meet this annual goal of 600,000 to 800,000 subsidized housing units would be to greatly expand the two low-income programs which incorporate the major advantages of the Boston experimental program—the Leasing and Rent Supplement Programs. Indeed, the potential advantages of the Rent Supplement Program were particularly stressed by the Committee on Urban Housing report:

The basic rent supplement approach, emphasizing flexible subsidies as well as private ownership, private financing, and private management, has many advantages. . . . This program can reach rather low income levels. If Congressional limits were removed, this program could serve the full range of families in need and could be used effectively by private business.[6]

This point about the restrictions on the Rent Supplements Program is an important one. As we suggested, our experimental program was not severely hemmed in by restrictions on housing amenities, subsidy percentages, construction costs or fair market rentals, family assets, and equity requirements for nonprofit sponsors. Not that there were no restrictions. There were. They were just generally more reasonable than the extensive list of congressional limits which have been tied to the Rent Supplement Program. Other changes too would enable the program to expand substantially; these would include such things as allowing full-fledged profit-making private business to build the housing—not just nonprofit or limited profit sponsors. As of this writing, the increasing combination of rent supplements with Section 236 apartment housing suggests that some of these earlier restrictions may be giving way; if this trend continues, the use of rent supplements for low-income families can be greatly expanded.

Thus in the United States the use of direct rent subsidies as an aid to the rehousing of poor families has added a promising alternative to public policy. The obvious attractions of rent subsidies—at least in the form of directly paying the difference between what a poor family can afford to spend on housing in the private market and the economic rent of a sound dwelling acceptable to them—are that they can go to work immediately so long as there is any sound housing on the market, that they can apply to widely scattered locations instead of concentrating the families in a few segregated neighborhoods, that they do not require a large capital investment, and yet can be used to encourage new construction by guaranteeing the rental of a certain number of units, and that they are not too difficult to administer. For the family displaced by urban renewal, rent subsidies can provide a choice beyond high-priced sound housing in the private market, lower-priced unsound housing in the private market, and lower-priced public housing. The family can be given a chance to live out in the city, in a good dwelling, without paying an exorbitant rent.

Direct rent subsidies are a fascinating experiment in housing policy. They are also a remarkable social experiment. They *can* be used in middle-income projects to promote the desegregation of the poor.[a] If the poor happen to be blacks, they may well promote a double desegregation—by color and by income. While some people claim that such desegregation is not only morally desirable but practically trouble free, others (even if committed to equal opportunity in housing) worry about the misunderstandings and irritations that might be produced by the living together of people differing in occupation, education, income, and style of life. Because segregation by occupation, education, income, and style of life is quite effective in American cities, as a matter of fact neither party has many examples of this sort of desegregation to praise or blame. Rent subsidies can permit poor people to live near others not so poor. They therefore set up a social experiment that students of cities ought to watch closely. If the subsidies are used in the relocation of families displaced by urban renewal, the experiment takes on an

---

[a]One additional problem currently being ligated concerns the increasing trend in some areas to build projects *exclusively* for rent supplements families, thus concentrating them in the heart of ghetto areas. See Shannon v. U.S. Department of Housing and Urban Development, 436 F. 2d 809 (1970).

added importance; it offers an opportunity to find out how much of the malaise of relocation is due to housing problems as such and how much is due to the changes in social relations that the moving about forces on families.

In fitting direct rent subsidies of the type involved in the Boston experimental program into the whole array of available means to assure that every poor family has sound housing and maximum freedom of choice, the framers of public policy face two major decisions and ought to keep several features of the housing market in mind when making them. The first decision is between full public ownership, on the one hand, and direct rent subsidies (including leasing arrangements) in the private market, on the other. The second is between the use of housing already available and the creation of new dwellings. Public ownership seems to gain in attractiveness when the demand for publicly-subsidized housing is relatively constant; direct rent subsidies, when that demand is variable or rising dramatically. Available housing is most likely to meet public needs when vacancy rates and turnover are high, discriminatory barriers few, and the average quality of housing good; new construction makes greater sense in cases of tight markets, extensive discrimination, and low housing quality. Direct rent subsidies in existing housing are therefore likely to work best where demand for publicly subsidized housing is variable, the housing stock good, discrimination weak, and the market relatively loose.

A program like the one tried in Boston—combining rent subsidies with the earmarking of newly constructed units—is likely to reach its maximum effectiveness where the housing market is tight and discriminatory, the housing stock inferior, and the demand either somewhat less variable or far greater than can be met with current public resources. Many American cities will come close to this last set of conditions for some years to come. For that reason, a program of direct rent subsidies tied to the construction of new dwellings through below-market interest rate arrangements should become a *major* feature of American housing and renewal policy. We should complement such a program with the construction or purchase of scattered-site public housing (for households with special needs, and perhaps as a hedge against cutbacks in the public funds available for housing) and with a flexible program of leasing in the existing private market by local housing authorities (to meet the most variable part of the demand for public subsidized housing). Such programs ought to include the option for the tenant to remain, at full rent, if his income rises above the ceiling and to buy his dwelling at a fair market price if he acquires the capital. American cities could reasonably devote half the money available for increasing the stock of publicly subsidized housing toward programs of direct rent subsidies in the private market.

If Boston's experience is a reliable sign, then large-scale investment in rent subsidies would work to the advantage of most of the people concerned. It would be easy to administer. Most important of all, it would give poor families the housing they need and prefer.

Appendix:
Before-Move
Interview Schedule

H1. First I would like to get a few facts about you and your family, so that I can have a picture of your present family situation -- things like the names, ages, and so forth, of each member of the family.
  (LIST FAMILY MEMBERS AS FOLLOWS:
  a. RESPONDENT
  b. SPOUSE
  c. CHILDREN
  d. OTHER RELATIVES OR BOARDERS IN THE HOUSEHOLD)

Name	Sex	Place of Birth	Year of Birth	Single, Married or divorced	Relation-ship	Occupation at Present	Education (Last grade completed)
a.							
b.							
c.							
d.							

HOUSING

Now, I have a few questions about housing.

H2. When did you move into this place? month _____ year _____

H3. Do you own this place, rent, or what? /own/ /buying/ /rent/ /janitor/

/with friends or relatives/ Other, SPECIFY_____

H4. How many rooms do you have? (Circle) 1 2 3 4 5 6 7 8 9 10+

H5. How much do
you pay a
month?

$_____

(a) IF OWN   1. Do you have any other regular expenses
    BUYING   for housing?
    JANITOR   /no/   /yes/

    IF YES: 1a. What is that? _____

    _____

    1b. How much is that?

    _____

(b) IF   1. Is that furnished or unfurnished?
                 / F / / U /

              2. Does that include heat? /No /   /Yes /

                 IF NO: 2a. How much is that?

              3. $_____

              3. Does that include gas and electricity?

                 /gas/ /no gas/ /elec/ /no elec/

                 IF NO: 3a. How much is that?

                              $_____

              4. When things go wrong around this place,
                 how well does the landlord (manager)
                 take care of repairs?

    /takes care of all/ /takes care of some/ /does little/

    /does nothing/ /don't know/ /not applicable/

H6. How did you find this place?   /Real Estate man/   /newspaper ad/

Other, SPECIFY_____

H7. How long did you look before you found this place?

/week or less/   /2-4 weeks/   /5 weeks - 6 months/   /7-12 months/

/year or more/   /don't know/   Other, SPECIFY_____

H8. Did you look at any other places before you moved into this one?

/yes/   /no/

IF YES: | H8a. How many?   (CIRCLE)   1 2 3 4 5 6-10 11 or more

H8b. How did you find out about those places (that place)?
Did any agencies or organizations help you look?

_____

_____

Hc. Why did you choose this place instead of the other(s)?

_____

_____

H9. Are you looking for another place now?   /yes/   /no/

Other: SPECIFY_____

IF YES: | H9a. How many places have you looked at?

(CIRCLE)   0 1 2 3 4 5 6-10 11 or more

H9b. Have any agencies or organizations helped you look?

/yes/   /no/

IF YES: H9c. Which ones?_____

_____

H9d. Have you decided on a place yet?   /yes/   /no/

BE SURE TO
GET   EXACT   IF YES: Where is that?_____
ADDRESS

H10. What do you think most people would say about the way this neighborhood looks in general? Would they call it very nice, fairly nice, nothing special, fairly bad, or very bad?

/very nice/ /fairly nice/ /nothing special/ /fairly bad/ /very bad/

/don't know/

H11. What do you think most people would say about the way this building looks on the outside?

/very nice/ /fairly nice/ /nothing special/ /fairly bad/ /very bad/

/don't know/

H12. Would you say you like this place very much, fairly well, all right, not too well, or not at all?

/very much/ /fairly well/ /all right/ /not too well/ /not at all/

/don't know/

H13. Do you expect to be living in this apartment (house) five years from now?

/yes/ /no/ /uncertain/

IF YES/UNCERTAIN:

IF NO:

H13a. If you ever had to move from this area, what things around here would you miss especially?

H13b. When you move, what things around here will you miss especially

H14. Here is a list of several parts of the Boston area (HAND CARD TO
RESPONDENT). Just assume you could find a place you liked for a
reasonable amount of money in any one of them. Which one would
you like to live in most? Which one next? Next? Which one least?
(CHECK BELOW)

	RANK				
	1	2	3	LEAST	COMMENTS
Braintree					
Brookline					
Cambridge					
Framingham					
Jamaica Plain					
Lexington					
Malden					
Newton					
Watertown					

H15. Where was the last place you lived before this one? (IN BOSTON, GET
NUMBER AND STREET: OUTSIDE OF BOSTON, GET LOCATION WITHIN STATE.
GO BACK TO 1 JANUARY, 1959.)

Last place	From when to when (Dates)	Was it a House Apt.		Why did you move from there?
1.	From ___ To			
2. Where did you live before that?	From ___ To			
3. Where did you live before that?	From ___ To			
4. Where did you live before that?	From ___ To			

Last place	From when to when (Dates)	Was it a House Apt.		Why did you move from there
5. Where did you live before that?	From ——— To			
6. Where did you live before that?	From ——— To			
7. Where did you live before that?	From ——— To			

(IF RESPONDENT BORN OUTSIDE BOSTON AND 1/1/59 ADDRESS IN BOSTON AREA)

H15a. When did you first come to the Boston Area? month_____ year_____

NEIGHBORHOOD

Now, I would like to ask you a few questions about this community:

N1a. Do you think of this area where you live as a neighborhood?

/yes/   /no/   /not sure/

    b. Why?_____

    _____

N2. If someone asked you what part of Boston you lived in, what would you say?

/Don't know/   /no name/   Other: SPECIFY_____

N3a. If you had to give someone directions to your house, what places, streets, or buildings would you use as landmarks?

_____

_____

/none/

N3b. Are there any streets or buildings which you think of as boundaries of this area?

_____

_____

_____

_____

/none/

N4. Now I'm going to read a list of things people sometimes think about when they move, and I'd like you to tell me whether you like this place better than the last place you lived, or don't like it as much, or think that there's not much difference, on each item. (PUT A CHECK IN THE PROPER SPACE.)

Compared to the last place you lived, do you like better, worse or the same:	Like it Better	Don't like it as much	Not much Difference
a. the size of this place			
b. the outside of the building			
c. the amount of rent you pay			
d. amount of space you have to invite your friends over			
e. amount of space you have to be by yourself when you want to			
f. as a place to bring up children			
g. grocery stores			
h. nearness to public transportation			
i. nearness to your church			
j. places to go for entertainment			
k. schools			
l. the class of people who live near you			
m. the safety of the street			
n. the quietness of the street			

N5a. When you moved into this area, how hard did you find it to get settled?

/very easy/   /easy/   /just like any other place/   /hard/   /very hard/

b. Why was that?_____

_____

_____

N6. How many of the names of your neighbors do you know?

/none/   /one or two/   /three to five/   /six or more/

N7. How many of your neighbors' apartments (or homes) have you been in during the last six months?

/none/   /one or two/   /three to five/   /six or more/

N8. How many of your neighbors do you talk with often?

/none/   /one or two/   /three to five/   /six or more/

N9. Now, about your friends. Who is the friend you get together with most often? Where does he (she) live? How often do you get together with him (her)? Is there anyone else you see often? Where does he (she) live? How often do you get together with him (her)? (REPEAT UNTIL RESPONDENT STOPS NAMING.)

Friend	Resident	Frequency

N10. Do you or anybody else in the household have any close relatives (like parents, uncles, cousins) in the Boston Area?

/yes/ /no/

IF YES: Who are they? Where do they live? How often do you see them?
(ASK FOR INFORMATION ON EACH HOUSEHOLD OF RELATIVES.)

Relationship	Resident	How often do you see them?

Some people say urban renewal has been good for this area and some say it has been bad.

N11. In general, would you say that this area is better off because of urban renewal, worse off because of it, or that it really doesn't make much difference?

/better off/   /worse off/   /not much difference/

Comments: _____
_____

N12. What do you think are the best things urban renewal has done for the people around here? (DO NOT READ BOXES)

/torn down bad housing/   /put up better housing/ /removed undesirable people/

Other, SPECIFY_____

_____

_____

N13. What do you think are the worst things urban renewal has done to the people around here? (DO NOT READ BOXES)

/forced people to move/   /started another slum/   /new housing too expensive/

Other, SPECIFY:_____

_____

_____

STATUS AND ASPIRATIONS

(IF COMMUNITY IS NOT ROXBURY, INSERT THE APPROPRIATE COMMUNITY NAME, SUCH AS CAMBRIDGE, ETC.)

C1. Some people like to think about others according to which class they are in. Even though you and I may not think of people this way, in which class would you say that most people in Roxbury fit?
(IF RESPONDENT IS UNABLE TO RESPOND OR USES DIFFERENT CATEGORIES, SAY: the ones I have listed are lower class, working class, middle class and upper class. IF RESPONDENT SAYS "DON'T KNOW" OR "ALL CLASSES", PROBE: Which one of them would most people in Roxbury fit into best?)

/lower class/   /working class/   /middle class/   /upper class/   /don't know/

Other: SPECIFY_____

C2. And in which class would you say most people in your present neighborhood fit? (USE INSTRUCTIONS ABOVE IF NECESSARY.)

/lower class/   /working class/   /middle class/   /upper class/   /don't know/

C3. In which class would you say that most people in your <u>old</u> neighborhood (last address) fit? (USE INSTRUCTIONS ABOVE IF NECESSARY.)

/lower class/ /working class/ /middle class/ /upper class/ /don't know/

C4. And how about yourself, if you were fitting yourself into one of these classes that some people talk about: where would you put yourself? (USE INSTRUCTIONS ABOVE IF NECESSARY.)

/lower class/ /working class/ /middle class/ /upper class/ /don't know/

C5a. Would you now tell me which of the following things is the most important in deciding the social standing of a person in this community? (SHOW CARD TO RESPONDENT)

/don't know/ /depends on person/ /rejects class/

	MOST	NEXT	LEAST
1. racial group			
2. the work he does			
3. having a lot of friends			
4. his wages or income			
5. his education			
6. the lightness of his skin			

b. Which of these is the next most important? (READ ALTERNATIVES AND CHECK ABOVE UNDER HEADING "NEXT".)

c. And which of these is the least important? (READ ALTERNATIVES AGAIN AND CHECK UNDER HEADING "LEAST".)

C6a. Is there any group of people around here who "stick together" and see themselves as better than their neighbors?

/yes/ /no/ /don't know/

b. IF YES: Who are they?_____

c. IF YES: Where do they live?_____

d. IF YES: Why do you think they act that way?_____
_____

Now then, let me ask you a few questions about your family and your children.

C7. What was the last grade in school which your mother completed? _____

C8. What kind of work was she doing when you were about sixteen?

_____

C9. What was the last grade in school which your father completed? _____

C10. Did your father live with you when you were growing up? /yes/ /no/

C11. What kind of work was he doing when you were about sixteen?

_____

C12. What kind of work did your father's father do?_____

_____

(CHECK PAGE 1 FOR LAST GRADE COMPLETED BY RESPONDENT.)

C13a. I see from what you told me earlier that you completed the _____ grade.
Did you want more schooling at the time you left school?

/yes/ /no/

b. IF YES: What kept you from getting more schooling?_____

_____

_____

C14a. (FOR RESPONDENTS WITH CHILDREN)

(1) Through what grade do you want to send your children?

_____

(2) How good are the chances for sending your children through that grade?

/very good/ /fairly good/ /poor/ /very poor/

(3) Do you want your children's lives to be different from your own? Would you say their lives should be different in many ways, different in just a few ways, or not different at all?

_____   _____   _____
/in many ways/   /in a few ways/   /not at all/

(4) What is the most important way in which you would like your children's lives to be different from your own life?

_____

_____

C14b. (FOR RESPONDENTS WITHOUT CHILDREN)

(1) If you had children of your own, through what grade would you want to send them?

_____

C15a. Now I would like to ask you about a certain situation: Suppose a boy of seventeen is doing very well in school and would be able to go to college on a scholarship. But, if he goes to college, it will mean leaving most of his buddies and not seeing his family very often. What will he probably do? (NOTE TO INTERVIEWER: IF RESPONDENT DOES NOT GIVE A CLEAR ANSWER OF "HE'LL DO THIS OR THAT," THAT IS, IF RESPONDENT SAYS "HE HAS TO MAKE UP HIS OWN MIND" OR "HE SHOULD DO . . . ", ASK AGAIN: WHAT WILL HE MOST LIKELY DO?)

_____

_____

b. Why do you say that?

_____

_____

C16. Just suppose you could afford to live anywhere you wanted to. I'll read you a list of places, and then ask you to tell me whether you'd like to live there, or not like to live there, or whether it wouldn't make much difference to you. (RESPONDENT MAY CHECK LAST COLUMN AS WELL AS PREFERENCE COLUMNS.)

If you had a completely free choice, would you like to live in:

	Like to	Not Like to	Not much difference	It Depends (WRITE IN QUALIFICATION)
a. an apartment in Roxbury				
b. an apartment somewhere else in the city				
c. a public housing development				
d. an apartment in the suburbs				
e. one of the new housing developments in Roxbury like Marksdale Gardens				
f. a house in Roxbury				
g. a house somewhere else in the city				
h. a house in the suburbs				
i. in the country				

PERSONAL INVENTORY

A1. Statements are often made about life in general. Would you tell me if you strongly agree, tend to agree, tend to disagree, or strongly disagree with the following: (GIVE CARD TO RESPONDENT)

(NOTE: PUT A CHECK IN THE APPROPRIATE COLUMN)

	Agree Strongly	Tend to Agree	Tend to Disagree	Strongly Disagree
a. No matter how hard you try, there's not much you can do to make a real change for the better.				
b. It's better to look on the bright side of things and not to be blue all the time.				
c. Sometimes I feel uneasy and sort of afraid without knowing exactly why.				
d. Things will get better only if you actually get out and do something to make them better.				

	Strongly Agree	Tend to Agree	Tend to Disagree	Strongly Disagree
e. It's hardly fair to bring a child into the world the way things look for the future.	___	___	___	___
f. Children should be spanked when they do something wrong.	___	___	___	___
g. Children who ask should be taught about sex at an early age.	___	___	___	___

A2. Here are some statements about intergroup relations. Would you please tell me if you strongly agree, tend to agree, tend to disagree, or strongly disagree, as I read each statement to you? (GIVE CARD TO RESPONDENT; IF RESPONDENT ONLY SAYS "AGREE" OR "DISAGREE", ASK HIM (OR HER) TO PICK ONE OF THE FOUR ALTERNATIVES ON THE CARD.)
(BE SURE TO STRESS UNDERLINED WORDS, SUCH AS NOT.)

	Strongly Agree	Tend to Agree	Tend to Disagree	Strongly Disagree
a. Young people should be allowed to marry whomever they want, regardless of race.	___	___	___	___
b. Integration is moving too fast in this country.	___	___	___	___
c. Most Negroes think more of themselves since the African countries became independent.	___	___	___	___
d. It is all right for some Negroes to do loud and noisy singing in church.	___	___	___	___
e. Negroes are always shouting about their rights, but they do not have much to offer the country.	___	___	___	___
f. Lower class Negroes should be allowed to live in this neighborhood.	___	___	___	___
g. Whites should be forced, if necessary, to give Negroes equal rights.	___	___	___	___
h. Negroes should not have their own special magazines like Ebony and Jet.	___	___	___	___

	Strongly Agree	Tend to Agree	Tend to Disagree	Strongly Disagree
i. Negroes blame white people for their troubles, but it is really their own fault.	___	___	___	___
j. Most white people want to see Negro Americans get equal rights.	___	___	___	___
k. A light Negro has a right to pass for white.	___	___	___	___
l. If Negroes push too hard for their rights, they may lose what they have gained so far.	___	___	___	___
m. Negroes are a lot better off today than they were five years ago.	___	___	___	___
n. White women should not date Negro men.	___	___	___	___
o. It is all right for Negroes to be loud and noisy around white people.	___	___	___	___
p. Roxbury's schools need to be made better before we worry about integrating them.	___	___	___	___
q. Negroes should not go into stores where they know they are not wanted.	___	___	___	___

(NOTE TO INTERVIEWER: ASK FOLLOWING ITEMS ONLY TO NEGRO RESPONDENTS.)

	Strongly Agree	Tend to Agree	Tend to Disagree	Strongly Disagree
r. If you don't have to, it is a good thing not to have too much contact with white people.	___	___	___	___
s. I feel that discrimination has hurt me personally.	___	___	___	___
t. I like to be called a "Negro."	___	___	___	___
u. I would like to get even with the white man for some of the things he has done to Negroes.	___	___	___	___
v. Sometimes, I hate white people.	___	___	___	___
w. Negroes should sing the old spirituals.	___	___	___	___
x. It is a good idea to trade in colored stores when you can.	___	___	___	___

	Strongly Agree	Tend to Agree	Tend to Disagree	Strongly Disagree
y. The trouble with most white people is that they think they are better than other people.	___	___	___	___
z. Sometimes, I dislike being a Negro.	___	___	___	___
aa. Light-skinned Negro women have an easier time in getting Negro men to date them.	___	___	___	___

A3. Would you prefer to live in a neighborhood where almost everyone is a Negro, almost everyone is white, or in a mixed neighborhood?

/all Negro/   /all white/   /mixed/   /it makes no difference/

(NOTE TO INTERVIEWER: IN ITEMS A4-A8 READ "WHITE" IF RESPONDENT IS NEGRO; READ "NEGRO" IF RESPONDENT IS WHITE.)

A4a. Now I would like to ask about your school years. Did you ever go to school with (white, Negro) children?

/yes/   /no/

b. IF YES: About how many of the students in the elementary school which you attended were (white, Negro)? Would you say a few, more than a few but less than half, or more than half?

/none/   /a few/   /more than a few but less than half/   /more than half/

Other, SPECIFY _____

(ASK A5 ONLY OF RESPONDENTS WITH CHILDREN)

A5. About how many of the students which your oldest child now goes to school with are (white, Negro)? Would you say a few, more than a few but less than half, or more than half?

/none/   /a few/   /more than a few but less than half/   /more than half/

Other, SPECIFY_____

A6. (NOTE: IF RESPONDENT IS A HOUSEWIFE, INSERT "YOUR HUSBAND WORKS" FOR "YOU WORK" IN THE FOLLOWING QUESTION.)

About how many of the people you (your husband) work with are (white, Negro)? Would you say a few, more than a few but less than half, or more than half?

/none/ /a few/ /more than a few but less than half/ /more than half/

Other, SPECIFY_____

A7. How often do (white, Negro) people visit in your home socially?

/once a week or more/ /once or twice a month/ /every few months/

/once or twice a year/ /never/

Other, SPECIFY_____

A8. Now I would like to know your personal feelings about the following situations.

Do you think you would find it a little unpleasant:

a. to eat at the same table with a (white, Negro) person? /yes/ /no/

b. to dance with a (white, Negro) person? /yes/ /no/

c. to go to a party where most of the people are (white, Negro)? /yes/ /no/

d. to have a (white, Negro) person for your very best friend? /yes/ /no/

e. to have a (white, Negro) person marry someone in your family? /yes/ /no/

f. to belong to a social club most members of which were (white, Negro)? /yes/ /no/

A9. What organizations in Boston do you feel have done the most for the Negro?

/don't know/ /NAACP/ /CORE/ Others, SPECIFY_____

_____

_____

A10. What kind of Negro leader do you admire most: one who constantly fights for civil rights of Negroes or one who disregards the race problem and works on general improvements that benefit the Negro community?

/one who fights for rights/   /one who works on community improvement/

/neither/   /don't know/   /both equally/

(ASK ITEMS A 11 - A 15 ONLY IF NEGRO RESPONDENTS.)

A11a. When was the last time you were reminded of your color? (GET SPECIFIC ANSWER.)

_____

_____

b. What happened?_____

_____

_____

A12. Are you proud to be a "Negro"?   /yes/   /no/   /don't know/

Why is that?_____

_____

_____

A13. How often do you read Negro magazines: would you say every week, most weeks, only occasionally, or not at all?

/every week/   /most weeks/   /occasionally/   /not at all/

A14. Do you think the Negro magazines try too hard or not hard enough to make Negroes want to fight for their rights?

/too hard/   /about right/   /not hard enough/

Other, SPECIFY_____

174

A15. (NOTE: IF RESPONDENT DOES NOT LIVE IN ROXBURY, INSERT APPROPRIATE
COMMUNITY NAME IN FOLLOWING QUESTION.)

Which of these two people do you think you have more in common to talk
about with? A white person who lives in Roxbury, or a Negro person
who lives in, say, Washington, D.C.

/white person here/   /Negro in Washington/

PARTICIPATION

P1. Now I would like to know about some of your activities. Will you please
tell me the names of the groups or organizations you belong to or attend.
(AFTER EACH GROUP OR ORGANIZATION IS NAMED, ASK QUESTIONS a-d IN ORDER.
ASK FOR EACH TYPE OF ORGANIZATION IN TURN.)

Type of Organization	Are you a member? (a)	How often do you attend? (b)	Do you contribute? (c)	Are you an officer or committee member? (d)
Religious (DO NOT ASK DENOMINATION)				
Civic				
Business, Union, or Professional				
Social or Recreational				

P2. Have you, or has anyone else in your family, had much to do with any of the following places in the last year? (IN EACH CASE NOTE ALL PERSONS HAVING CONTACT.)

	Respondent	Spouse	Children	Other (SPECIFY)	None
a. Boston City Hospital					
b. Norfolk House					
c. Blue Hill Protestant Ctr.					
d. Charles Street Church					
e. Boston Public Library					
f. Freedom House					
g. Roxbury Boy's Club					
h. St.Mark's Social Center					

P3. If you needed advice on a serious financial problem, what would you do?

/don't know/ /handle it myself/ /see a friend/ /see a relative/

/neighbor/ /social agency official/ /lawyer/ /religious official/

/political official/ /bank/ /loan company/ /printed source/

Other, SPECIFY _____

P4. Have you voted in a local or national election in the last four years?

/yes/ /no/

P5. Now then, I would like to ask you about statements that some people make; please tell whether you strongly agree with them, tend to agree, tend to disagree, or strongly disagree. (SHOW CARD WITH RESPONSES)

	Strongly Agree	Tend to Agree	Tend to Disagree	Strongly Disagree
a. American is truly a land of opportunity and anyone can get ahead if he works hard enough.				
b. The federal government should see to it that every person has a decent and steady job.				

	Strongly Agree	Tend to Agree	Tend to Disagree	Strongly Disagree
c. Government medical care for poor and aged American citizens would be a good thing.	___	___	___	___
d. People who are communists should not be allowed to speak at schools and clubs.	___	___	___	___
e. The U.S. government should quit meddling with the affairs of foreign countries and tend to its own problems at home.	___	___	___	___
f. Most politicians really do not care about me and my family.	___	___	___	___
g. Security is what I want most out of a job.	___	___	___	___

P6. Now, I'd like to get an idea of your activities on a typical day. Let's start with the beginning of the day. (IF INTERVIEW IS ON SUNDAY OR MONDAY, SAY: Friday. IF INTERVIEW IS TUESDAY THROUGH SATURDAY, SAY: yesterday), and put down everything you did for 15 minutes or more. What were you doing at 6 in the morning? Until when? What did you do then? Until when? (MARK START AND FINISH OF EACH ACTIVITY AT LEFT MARGIN. IF TWO ACTIVITIES AT ONCE (EXAMPLE: HOUSEWORK and TELEVISION) USE TWO COLUMNS.)

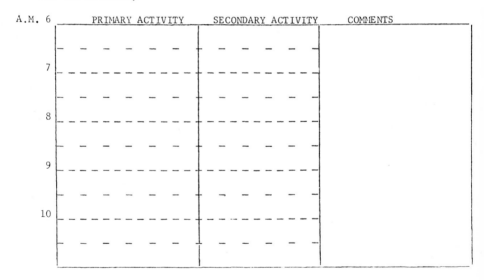

A.M. 11	PRIMARY ACTIVITY	SECONDARY ACTIVITY	COMMENTS
NOON			
P.M. 1			
2			
3			
4			
5			
6			
7			
8			
9			
10			
11			
MIDNIGHT			

PROBE: Did you talk on the phone or spend 15 minutes or more with anyone that you haven't mentioned? When was that? Did you do any reading, listening to the radio or watching television that you haven't mentioned? When was that?

P7a. Day of the week reported on _____

  b. Would you say this was about like most days?   /yes/ /no/

  c. IF NO: Why is that? _____

_____

WORK INFORMATION

Now, I'd like to ask some questions about the work you were doing last week.

01. Were you /working/   or   /not working/ ?

02. (IF NOT WORKING) Are you   (READ ALTERNATIVES):

  /housewife/ /looking for work/ /retired/ /disabled/ /on temporary/
                                                            / lay off /
  Other: SPECIFY_____

03. (IF HOUSEWIFE ASK)

  a. Where does your husband work?_____

_____

  b. Exactly what kind of work does he do now?

_____

_____

  c. When did he start his present job? _____

04. (IF RESPONDENT WAS WORKING OR ON TEMPORARY VACATION ASK)

  a. Where do you work?_____

_____

b. Exactly what kind of work do you do now?_____

_____

_____

c. When did you start your present job?_____month _____year

05. About how much was your family income from all sources, after taxes, in the year 1963? $_____

IF FIGURE GIVEN	IF RESPONDENT IS UNCERTAIN

IF FIGURE GIVEN

Could you give me a rough breakdown of where that came from?

Head $_____

Other earners $_____

Rents $_____

Social Security $_____

Welfare $_____

Other $_____

(SPECIFY)_____

IF RESPONDENT IS UNCERTAIN

Maybe we could work it out this way. Who was earning money last year? About how much pay did he take home a week when he was working? About how many weeks did he work? Anybody else?

EARNER	PAY/WEEK	WEEKS WORKED	TOTAL

Did your family have any other source of income? What was it? How much was that? Any other income?

SOURCE	AMOUNT/WEEK	WEEKS	TOTAL

Revised Total $ _____

(IF RESPONDENT REFUSES ASK): Was it over $6,000?   /yes/   /no/

06. Do you expect your income this year to be about the same?

/yes/ /no/ /don't know/

IF NO: About how much this year? $_____

Why is that?_____

_____

_____

07a. Let's think about exactly a year from now. What is the best job situation you could hope to be in by then?

_____

_____

b. Could you explain how that would happen?_____

_____

c. Would you say that the chances of that are good?

/yes/   /no/

08a. What is the best housing situation?_____

_____

b. How would that happen?_____

_____

c. Would you say the chances of that are good?

/yes/   /no/

09. People often make decisions that affect their lives for some time to come such as quitting a job, getting married or divorced, leaving or going back to school, and many other choices.

a. What was the last big choice like that you made?

/none/   /don't know/

SPECIFY:_____

_____

b. When was that? _____month _____year

c. If you had to make that choice again, how do you think you would make it?

/same way/   /different way/

SPECIFY:_____

_____

O10a. What is the next big choice or decision you expect to make?

(IF RESPONSE IS "BIG DECISION" ASK b, c, and d. IF RESPONSE IS "DON'T KNOW" or "NONE", ask d ONLY.)

/don't know/   /none/   /big decision/

SPECIFY_____

_____

b.When will that happen?_____

c.How do you think you'll choose?_____

_____

d.Why is that?_____

_____

(READ TO RESPONDENT)

That concludes the interview. We are studying the problems of housing and urban renewal in the Boston area and are interviewing a large number of people to find out how they feel on these questions. We are grateful for your help, and we may see you again in several months, because we will be re-interviewing some people to find out about changes in housing in this area. This project will help all of us in America to better deal with the problems of living in cities.

INTERVIEWER'S REPORT

(COMPLETE AFTER LEAVING RESPONDENT)

1. Respondent's address: Number _____ Street_____

   Apartment No._____Floor_____ Entry No._____

2. Race: /white/   /Negro/

3. (IF NEGRO) Would you describe Respondent as:

   a.   /dark/   /medium/   /light/

   b.   /stout/   /medium build/   /thin/

4. General comments on Interview and Respondent:

   Responsiveness (volume of information volunteered, amount of probing
   required, etc.)

   /overly responsive/   /very responsive/   /moderately responsive/

   /relatively unresponsive/   /very unresponsive/   /refusal/

   Comments:

   _____

   _____

   _____

   _____

5 a. Special circumstances of interview.
     Who else was present besides the respondent?

   _____

   _____

   _____

   _____

b. How much did they participate in answering the questions?

_____

_____

_____

_____

_____

c. In what part of the house did you conduct the interview?

_____

_____

_____

d. Were there any important interruptions or distractions?
   What were they?

_____

_____

_____

_____

_____

e. Note any questions with which the respondent had great difficulty.

_____

_____

_____

_____

_____

6. Type of Building (CHECK APPROPRIATE BLANKS)

Single House   _____
2 Family   _____
3-6 Family   _____
7 or more   _____
Public Housing   _____
221 (d) 3   _____
Apartment in a House _____
Furnished Rooms   _____
Don't Know   _____

7. Condition of Dwelling Unit (housekeeping)

Neat and clean to extreme   _____
Neat and clean, but lived in look   _____
Somewhat disorderly, but probably
   temporarily so   _____
Very disorderly and probably not
   temporarily so   _____

(CIRCLE NUMBER WHICH IS MOST APPROPRIATE IN QUESTIONS 8-11)

8. Condition of Dwelling Area:

1.	2.	3.	4.	5.
Dump, slums tenements; or dwelling units are very few compared to factories, warehouses or non-dwelling functions, etc. Any area which is in general run-down deteriorated	Factories business, etc., but still half or more of units are dwelling units however general appearance is poor, yards are dirty, small, have trash in, homes are not well kept.	In general a residential section though there may be neighborhood stores serving the area; is not a general zone of transition unless a new development, streets are paved.	All residential; houses well kept, unless a new development streets paved yards may be small but are well taken care of.	All residential; large yards; no congestion; homes range from average to good or excellent with most of them good or excellent; lots are large, etc.

9. Condition of Dwelling Unit (Ceiling, Walls):

1.	2.	3.
No major or minor repairs needed.	Some minor repairs needed, but otherwise all right.	Major repairs needed

10. Condition of Dwelling Unit (roof, steps, chimney, siding, etc.):

1.	2.	3.	4.	5.
Not one, but several basic items are in need of repair or were makeshift to begin with.	One or two basic items in need of repair but otherwise dwelling shows only general wear.	Not more than one basic item in need of repair and rest of dwelling in good condition or no basic items in need of repair but show wear and discoloration.	Basic items show no need of repair and there is no sign of their becoming so in the near future; there is little sign of wear.	Basic items not in need of repair nor do they show much wear; the quality of material is high such as slate roof, cooper spouting stonework, etc.

11. Structure:

1.	2.	3.	4.	5.
Not a standard dwelling type; a shack, a barn, tent, etc.	Conventional frame with no landscaping, or old deteriorated brick, etc.	Conventional frame with yard and landscaping; custom frame, brick, stone, stucco, with small or no yard and landscaping.	Same as 3. except is well situated on a lot and has large size yard, is well landscaped and well cared for.	Same as preceding but is an "estate" -- has expansive landscape, etc.

12. Living Room Furnishings:

Books:
  None   ____
  1 foot or
    1 dozen   ____
  More   ____

Record player ____
Television ____
Radio ____
Family photos ____
Other pictures,
  mirrors,
  objects ____
Magazines ____
  (Titles)_____

Notes

Preface

1. This book is a revised version of an earlier mimeographed research report prepared on behalf of the Joint Center for Urban Studies of the Massachusetts Institute of Technology and Harvard University, Cambridge, Massachusetts. That report was entitled *Rent Supplements in Boston* (October, 1968). A brief article outlining certain of our basic findings and their policy implications appeared as Charles Tilly and Joe Feagin, "Boston's Experiment with Rent Subsidies," *Journal of the American Institute of Planners*, 323-329. We have drawn on this article in making our arguments here, particularly in Chapters 1 and 9.

Chapter 1
The Problem

1. National Commission on Urban Problems, *Building the City* (Washington, D.C.: U.S. Government Printing Office, 1968), p. 68.

2. Chester Hartman, "The Housing of Relocated Families," *Journal of the American Institute of Planners*, 30 (November 1964), 274.

3. Scott Greer, *Urban Renewal and American Cities* (New York: Bobbs-Merrill Co., 1965), p. 3.

4. President's Committee on Urban Housing, *A Decent Home* (Washington, D.C.: U.S. Government Printing Office, 1968), p. 61.

5. Ibid., p. 58.

6. Ibid., p. 59.

Chapter 2
The Housing of Boston's Population

1. *U.S. News and World Report*, September 21, 1964; *Engineering News-Record*, February 20, 1964; *Toronto Daily Star*, May 27, 1967.

2. The description of Boston's population is drawn largely from Charles Tilly, "Metropolitan Boston's Social Structure," in Richard Bolan, ed. *Issues and Problems of Boston Metropolitan Area Development* (Cambridge and Boston: Joint Center for Urban Studies of M.I.T. and Harvard for the Metropolitan Area Planning Council, 1965), Part III, pp. 1-31. 1970 census data are not yet available.

187

3. Frank L. Sweetser, *Patterns of Change in the Social Ecology of Metropolitan Boston, 1950-1960* (Boston: Massachusetts Department of Mental Health, 1962); and *The Social Ecology of Metropolitan Boston, 1960* (Boston: Massachusetts Department of Mental Health, 1962).

4. Frank L. Sweetser, "Factor Structure as Ecological Structure in Helsinki and Boston," *Acta Sociologica*, 8 (1965), 205-225.

5. Cf. Stanley Lieberson, *Ethnic Patterns in American Cities* (New York: Free Press, 1963).

6. *Analysis of the Boston, Massachusetts, Housing Market as of October 1, 1966* (Washington, D.C.: Department of Housing and Urban Development, Federal Housing Administration, October 1967), p. 38.

7. Ibid., p. 39.

8. *The General Plan for Boston, Preliminary Report* (Boston, 1952).

9. *Summary, 1965/1975 General Plan for the City of Boston* (Boston, 1964).

10. *1965/1975 General Plan for the City of Boston* (Boston, 1964).

11. Lewis G. Watts and others, *The Middle-Income Negro Family Faces Urban Renewal* (Waltham: Research Center of the Florence Heller Graduate School for Advanced Studies in Social Welfare, Brandeis University, for the Department of Commerce and Development, Commonwealth of Massachusetts, 1964).

12. Watts, p. 86.

13. Morton Rubin, "Resident Response to Urban Rehabilitation in a Negro Working Class Neighborhood," in Arthur B. Shostak and William Gomberg, eds., *Blue-Collar World* (Englewood Cliffs: Prentice-Hall, 1964), pp. 247-58.

14. Ibid., pp. 254-55.

15. See Karl E. Taueber and Alma F. Taueber, *Negroes in Cities* (Chicago: Aldine, 1965).

16. Chester Hartman, "The Housing of Relocated Families," *Journal of the American Institute of Planners*, 30 (November 1964), 267.

17. Boston Redevelopment Authority, "Family Relocation Progress Report, Washington Park Urban Renewal Area" (mimeographed, 1966).

18. Watts, *Middle-Income Negro Family*, pp. 101-12.

19. *Boston Globe*, May 7, 1966.

20. *Annual Report of the Massachusetts Commission against Discrimination, January 1, 1965 to December 31, 1965*, p. 31.

21. Ralph V. Conant, "An Evaluation of Fair Housing Incorporated, Boston, Massachusetts, September 1, 1963-August 31, 1965" (mimeographed, Joint Center for Urban Studies of the Massachusetts Institute of Technology and Harvard University, 1966).

22. *Annual Report of the Massachusetts Commission Against Discrimination*, 1965, p. 28.

23. May B. Hipshman, *Public Housing at the Crossroads: The Boston Housing Authority* (Boston: Citizens' Housing and Planning Association, 1967).

Chapter 3
Political Controversy over Rent Subsidies: The Emergence of the Rent Supplements Program

1. This message is reprinted in U.S., Congress, House Committee on Banking and Currency, *Housing and Urban Development Act of 1965*, Hearings, before a subcommittee of the Committee on Banking and Currency, House of Representatives, on H.R. 5840 and related bills (89th Cong., 1st sess., 1965), part I, pp. 67-74.

2. Ibid., part I, pp. 167ff.

3. Ibid., part I, pp. 245ff.

4. Ibid., part I, p. 280.

5. Ibid., part II, pp. 795-96.

6. Ibid., part I, pp. 548-49.

7. Ibid., part I, pp. 425ff. This opposition provoked heated criticism of public housing officials by several congressmen, especially in the Senate hearings.

8. Congressional Quarterly Service, *Housing a Nation* (Washington, D.C.: Congressional Quarterly, Inc., 1966), p. 75. Although President Johnson mentioned low-income families in his initial message, the draft bill and Weaver's House testimony limited the program to families whose incomes were too high for public housing, "middle-income" families to use Secretary Weaver's term.

9. This discussion is based on a privately published pamphlet reprinting the "Minority Views," entitled *Extract from Report No. 365, House of Representatives: Minority Views* (89th Cong., 1st sess., 1965).

10. The following discussion of the House debate is based on these sources: U.S., Congress, House (89th Cong., 1st sess., June 28, 1965) *Congressional Record*, CXI, pp. 1486 ff; U.S., Congress, House (89th Cong., 1st sess., June 29, 1965) *Congressional Record*, CXI, pp. 15128 ff; U.S., Congress, House (89th Cong., 1st sess., June 30, 1965), pp. 15217 ff. Discussion of congressional debates, unless otherwise noted, is based on the *Congressional Record.*

11. U.S., Congress, Senate, Committee on Education and Labor, *United States Housing Act of 1936, Hearings*, on S. 4424 (74th Cong., 2d sess., 1936), p. 249.

12. H.G. Hallenbeck, Jr., "Statement on Department of Housing and Urban Development and Independent Offices Appropriations for Fiscal Year 1967," presented before the Subcommittee on Independent Offices, House Committee on Appropriations, for the U.S. Chamber of Commerce, Washington, D.C., April 20, 1966, pp. 8, 10 (mimeographed).

13. U.S., Congress, Senate, Committee on Education and Labor, *United States Housing Act of 1936, Hearings*, p. 178.

14. Ibid., p. 168.

15. From private correspondence with NAREB, dated June 19, 1966, and February 13, 1968.

16. See, for example, U.S. Congress, House (89th Cong., 1st sess., June 28, 1965), *Congressional Record*, CXI, pp. 14868 ff.

17. Ibid., p. 14868.

18. Ibid., p. 14872.

19. See above, n. 7.

20. See, for example, U.S. Congress, House (89th Cong., 1st sess., June 28, 1965), *Congressional Record*, CXI, pp. 14878 ff.

21. Ibid., p. 14879.

22. Congressional Quarterly Service, *Congressional Quarterly Weekly Report*, week ending July 2, 1965, pp. 1269-70.

23. Ibid., pp. 1295-96; and U.S. Congress, Senate, Committee on Banking and Currency, *Housing Legislation of 1965, Hearings*, before a subcommittee of the Committee on Banking and Currency, Senate, on S. 1354 and related legislation (89th Cong., 1st sess., 1965). Most of the testimony presented to the Senate subcommittee was identical to that presented in the House. The Commissioner of the New York State Division of Housing and Community Renewal did make an interesting point in the Senate hearings; he noted that the federal rent subsidy program had been anticipated by a somewhat similar New York rental assistance program which had begun in the early part of 1965.

24. U.S. Congress, Senate (89th Cong., 1st sess., July 14, 1965), *Congressional Record*, CXI, pp. 16729 ff; U.S. Congress, Senate (89th Cong., 1st sess., July 15, 1965), *Congressional Record*, CXI, pp. 16906 ff.

25. Congressional Quarterly Service, *Congressional Quarterly Weekly Report*, week ending August 6, 1965, p. 12.

26. U.S. Congress, House, Committee on Banking and Currency, *Highlights of the Housing and Urban Development Act of 1965* (89th Cong., 1st sess., 1965), p. 1.

27. Ibid., pp. 1-3.

28. U.S. Congress, House (89th Cong., 1st sess., October 14, 1965), *Congressional Record*, CXI, p. 26978.

29. Ibid., p. 26979.

30. Ibid., pp. 26978 ff.

31. Congressional Quarterly Service, *Congressional Quarterly Weekly Report*, week ending October 22, 1965, p. 2122; and U.S. Congress, Senate (89th Cong., 1st sess., October 20, 1965), *Congressional Record*, CXI, pp. 27534 ff.

32. Congressional Quarterly Service, *Congressional Quarterly Weekly Report*, week ending February 18, 1966, p. 422.

33. Congressional Quarterly Service, *Congressional Quarterly Weekly Report*, week ending December 24, 1965, p. 2846.

34. U.S. Congress, House (89th Cong., 2d sess., February 25, 1966), *Congressional Record*, CXII, pp. 3954-55.

35. U.S. Congress, House (89th Cong., 2d sess., March 29, 1966), *Congressional Record*, CXII, pp. 6710 ff.

36. Ibid., pp. 6726-27.

37. Ibid., especially pp. 6727 ff.

38. Ibid., p. 6765.

39. Congressional Quarterly Service, *Congressional Quarterly Weekly Report*, April 8, 1966, p. 745.

40. Quoted in ibid., p. 745.

41. Ibid., pp. 746-47.

42. Ibid., p. 747.

43. Ibid.

44. U.S. Congress, Senate (89th Cong., 2d sess., April 27, 1966), *Congressional Record*, CXII, pp. 8656 ff.

45. Ibid., p. 8661.

46. Ibid., p. 8666.

47. Congressional Quarterly Service, *Congressional Quarterly Weekly Report*, April 29, 1966, p. 865.

48. Who were the proponents and opponents of the Rent Supplements Program during the 1965-66 roll call votes? Examining four key votes, including votes on initial authorization and appropriations, a *Congressional Quarterly*, analysis found that the program had a varying number of supporters, running from 208 to 162. No fewer than 62 congressmen voting on the amendment which finally provided funds for fiscal 1967 had changed their position at one time or another. Forty percent of those who switched finally voted against the amendment, while 60 percent finally voted for it. According to the *Congressional Quarterly* survey most of the "switchers" were from Southern and Western states, including such states as Texas, Georgia, California, Colorado, New Mexico, and Tennessee. Democratic representatives from large metropolitan areas, such as Chicago, Detroit, New York, Philadelphia, and Los Angeles generally voted in support of rent supplements. Very few Republicans supported the program; only 6 of the 125 Republicans voted for the last funding amendment. Thus support for the program came generally from Democrats—and particularly from Democrats representing urban areas in the North. Congressional Quarterly Service, *Congressional Quarterly Weekly Report*, October 14, 1966, p. 2485-86.

49. Congressional Quarterly Service, *Congressional Quarterly Weekly Report*, June 24, 1966, p. 1347.

50. U.S. Congress, House (89th Cong., 2d sess., May 10, 1966), *Congressional Record*, CXII, pp. 10215 ff; and U.S. Congress, Senate (89th Cong., 2d sess., August 10, 1966), *Congressional Record*, CXII, pp. 18903 ff.

51. Congressional Quarterly Service, *Congressional Quarterly Weekly Report*, August 12, 1966, p. 1754.

52. Congressional Quarterly Service, *Congressional Quarterly Weekly Report*, September 2, 1966, p. 1930.

53. Congressional Quarterly Service, *Congressional Quarterly Weekly Report*, November 11, 1966, pp. 2804-05.

54. U.S. Congress, House (90th Cong., 1st sess., May 16, 1967), *Congressional Record*, CXIII, pp. H5556 ff; U.S. Congress, House (90th Cong., 1st sess., May 17, 1967), *Congressional Record*, CXIII, pp. H5658 ff.

55. U.S. Congress, House (90th Cong., 1st sess., May 16, 1967), *Congressional Record*, CXIII, pp. H5556.

56. Ibid., p. H5563.

57. U.S. Congress, House (90th Cong., 1st sess., May 15, 1967), *Congressional Record*, CXIII, p. H5504.

58. U.S. Congress, Senate (90th Cong., 1st sess., September 20, 1967), *Congressional Record*, CXIII, pp. S13335 ff.

59. Ibid., p. S133350.

60. U.S. Congress, House (90th Cong., 1st sess., October 24, 1967), *Congressional Record*, CXIII, p. H13867 ff; U.S. Congress, House (90th Cong., 1st sess., October 26, 1967), *Congressional Record*, CXIII, pp. H14041 ff.

61. Congressional Quarterly Service, *Congressional Quarterly Weekly Report*, February 16, 1968, p. 292.

Chapter 4
The Boston Experiment and Its Evaluation

1. For a more general discussion of the problems of evaluation research, see Howard E. Freeman and Clarence C. Sherwood, "Research in Large-Scale Intervention Programs," *Journal of Social Issues*, 21 no. 1 (1965): 11-28.

2. This is a direct quotation from the BHA proposal to the Housing and Home Finance Agency.

Chapter 7
Social Life with and Without Rent Subsidies

1. Herbert Gans, *The Urban Villagers* (New York: Free Press, 1962); the whole literature is well reviewed in Marc Fried, "Functions of the Working-Class Community in Modern Urban Society: Implications for Forced Relocation," *Journal of the American Institute of Planners*, 33 (March, 1967), which includes information about the West End.

2. A more extensive discussion of this literature and of some aspects of the data discussed in this chapter can be found in Joe R. Feagin, "The Social Ties of Negro Urbanites," (Harvard University, unpublished Ph.D. dissertation, 1966); Joe R. Feagin, "The Kinship Ties of Negro Urbanites," *Social Science Quarterly*, 49 (1968), 660-665; and David C. Perry and Joe R. Feagin, "Stereotyping in Black and White," in *People and Politics in Urban Society*, ed. by Harlan Hahn (Beverly Hills, California, 1972), pp. 433-463.

Chapter 8
How the Program Worked . . . and What Difference It Made

1. See Commonwealth of Massachusetts, *Final Report of the Special Commission on Low-Income Housing* (Boston: Wright and Potter, 1964), pp. 54-61.

2. May B. Hipshman, *Public Housing at the Crossroads: The Boston Housing Authority* (Boston: Citizens' Housing and Planning Association, 1967), pp. 5-6.

Chapter 9
Low-Income Housing Programs: Review and Conclusions

1. In these opening paragraphs and at several other points in this chapter we draw heavily on the following previously published research article: Charles Tilly and Joe R. Feagin, "Boston's Experiment with Rent Subsidies," *Journal of the American Institute of Planners*, 36 (1970), 323-329.

2. This section draws heavily on reports and statistical sheets supplied by the Division of Research and Statistics, Federal Housing Administration, Department of Housing and Urban Development. We are grateful for published and unpublished data they have supplied to us.

3. See footnote 2 for source.

4. President's Committee on Urban Housing, *A Decent Home* (Washington, D.C.: U.S. Government Printing Office, 1968), p. 11.

5. Ibid., p. 8. (Italics have been omitted.)

6. Ibid., p. 65.

Index

195

About the Authors

Joe R. Feagin is Associate Professor of Sociology at the University of Texas (Austin). He took his Ph.D. in sociology from Harvard in 1966 and has taught at the University of Massachusetts (Boston) and the University of California, Riverside.

His primary teaching and research interests lie in the general areas of urban sociology and race relations; he is currently engaged in research on ghetto revolts, black political power in the South, and residential segregation.

Charles Tilly is professor of sociology and history at the University of Michigan. He has taught and held research appointments at the University of Delaware, Princeton, Harvard, M.I.T., the University of Toronto, the Center for Advanced Study in the Behavioral Sciences, and the Institute for Advanced Study. He performed his undergraduate and graduate work at Harvard and Oxford. Most of his work deals with urbanization, cities, and political change in Europe and North America. He is the author of *The Vendée*, a study of provincial response to the French Revolution.

Constance Willard Williams is a graduate of Berea College and the Boston University School of Social Work. Her current position is Assistant Professor of Liberal Studies and Social Work at Boston University.

She has done research in geriatrics, education, and housing. She has been a social worker at The James Jackson Putnam Children's Center in the Roxbury section of Boston.